THE
GLORY
OF THE
ENGLISH GARDEN

THE
GLORY
OF THE
ENGLISH GARDEN

MARY KEEN
PHOTOGRAPHS BY CLAY PERRY

A BULFINCH PRESS BOOK
LITTLE, BROWN AND COMPANY
BOSTON   TORONTO   LONDON

Right: William Kent, the creator of Rousham, once spent all night in the Temple at Chiswick enjoying the effects of the moon. Stagey sunsets and theatrical dawns would have been very much to his taste.

Page 1: The gardens at Athelhampton were subjected to a major restoration in the first few years of this century. The stone-edged lily pond in the Green Court was designed by Inigo Thomas, who was responsible for most of the work there.

Page 2: At Barnsley House, rare plants and British natives rub shoulders in the packed flower beds. Cowslips and primroses are allocated plenty of room and in spring the garden is a mass of bulbs. This dense mixture of exotics with wild flowers is typical of gardens of the last quarter of the twentieth century.

Page 3: The rose garden at Cliveden was designed by Geoffrey Jellicoe. In it, fluid island beds in Modern Movement shapes are linked by curving arches. The statues which stand among the roses are a legacy of William Waldorf Astor's Italianate taste.

First United States Edition
First published in Great Britain by Barrie & Jenkins Ltd.

Library of Congress Cataloging-in-Publication Data
Keen, Mary
      The glory of the English garden / Mary Keen : photographs by Clay Perry.
         p. cm.
      "A Bulfinch Press book."
      Includes index
      ISBN 0−8212−1761−5
      1. Gardens—England. 2. Gardens, English. 3. Gardens—England—Pictorial works.
      4. Gardens. English—Pictorial works. I. Perry, Clay.   II. Title.
      SB466.G75E554   1989
    712'.0941—dc20   89−12225
                                                                                        CIP

Bulfinch Press is an imprint and trademark of Little, Brown and Company (Inc.)

PRINTED AND BOUND IN ITALY BY AMILCARE PIZZI SPA

CONTENTS

Introduction   8

CHAPTER 1: KNOTS, HERBS & FLOWERY MEADS   11

CHAPTER 2: AVENUES, GROVES, GROTTOS & CANALS   33

CHAPTER 3: TEMPLES, IDYLLS & SERPENTINE CURVES   59

CHAPTER 4: CLUMPS, LAKES & WAGGONLOADS OF ACACIAS   89

CHAPTER 5: TERRACES, SHRUBBERIES, ROCKERIES & ROSES   111

CHAPTER 6: CARPETS OF COLOUR, FOLIAGE & FERNS   135

CHAPTER 7: BRIAR ROSES, LILIES, TOPIARY & BORDERS   163

CHAPTER 8: HEDGES, HERBS, HELLEBORES & GREENERY   197

CHAPTER 9: POTTAGE, PEAS, PEACHES & PINEAPPLES   237

APPENDIX: GARDENS FEATURED IN THE BOOK   248

BIBLIOGRAPHY   251

ACKNOWLEDGEMENTS   252

INDEX   253

INTRODUCTION

Chiswick House *by George Lambert (1742)*

ENGLISH GARDENS HAVE SUCH A TIMELESS QUALITY THAT THEY are not regarded as subjects for fashion. In the lumber room of memory, impressions of cottages with roses around the door and masses of hollyhocks are seen in one continuous tradition with green views and statues in long grass. Inside a house most people have some sense of period, but outside it is rare to have a clear idea of how varied English garden style has been. Herbals and old prints provide dusty glimpses into the past, but they give no sense of the green reality of a garden. They can never convey the air and space of those enchanted places, and to the uninitiated, they reveal very little about the lives of the people who enjoyed them.

The best way to approach garden history is not by looking at illustrations of what existed, but by seeing it on the ground. All this has been made much easier in the last twenty years, when the fragments of period gardens which remained have in many places been developed into full blown reconstructions. The National Trust has breathed new life into the land around its great houses and many private owners have also begun to imitate their example. On a smaller scale, occupants of minor period houses have started to be aware of the importance of making gardens to complement the houses they surround. On the whole, outdoor restorations are often more successful than those inside. Historic houses that are open to the public are used in very different ways from those for which they were intended. Shuffling around in a crowd, on a roped off route, is not at all the same as using a house for everyday life. In a garden it is different. Life goes on much as it always has done – you can walk the same paths and gaze at the same views as people did when the place was created. Flowers still smell as they used to hundreds of years ago, grass grows, trees shade and fountains fall, as they did for our ancestors. In no other art form is history so easy to absorb.

Looking at the layout of a period garden only gives half of the picture, however. The other half comes with understanding how people felt in those gardens. A knowledge of past hopes and aspirations will colour places which can seem dull when judged by present day standards. Visiting a garden can be transformed by understanding the importance of the towers of thought that went into the making of those early places.

Today, when most preoccupations out of doors are concerned with mowing the lawn, or growing vegetables, or choosing from a surfeit of hybridised plants, peoples' expectations of gardens are limited. In the twentieth century we appreciate only skill, space and variety. It was not always so. For approximately the last hundred years, gardens have been running on horticultural tramlines. The huge influx of plants in the middle of the last century distracted English garden makers from their early purpose, which was to translate into living form something of their inner lives. Gardens used to be about thoughts and aspirations; their intellectual horizons stretched far beyond their physical boundaries. This is the greatest change. The shift from garden-making to gardening has made it hard for us to gear our minds to the pace of thought in the past.

Period gardens are living proof of changing fashions. What gardens meant to their owners has differed in every century and they reveal as much about the character and preoccupations of the men and women who made them as any other art form. English gardens are about more than just the plants they contain. Their superficial beauty tends to be so spellbinding that most people are content to look no further, but understanding their meaning adds a magic all of its own. That is the real Glory of the English Garden.

MARY KEEN
BERKSHIRE
JUNE 1989

A S THIS BOOK TAKES THE FORM OF A HISTORY, I WOULD LIKE TO take this opportunity to make an observation about the current period in English garden history.

During the best part of the 1980s I have travelled throughout Britain, working on various photographic projects, mostly concerned with nature and the countryside. I have become increasingly aware that environmental pollution is taking a higher toll year by year. Many trees have already succumbed, and some of the gardens in this book are beginning to show symptoms.

It can only be a matter of time before the gardens as they are now will cease to exist. Unless something drastic is done within the very near future, these exquisite places will be lost for ever and will exist only in the memory and in the pages of books.

CLAY PERRY
LONDON
MAY 1989

CHAPTER 1
KNOTS, HERBS & FLOWERY MEADS

'Oh Paradise thy rival is this place'

Portrait of an unknown melancholy man *by Isaac Oliver*

T HE BEST GARDENS IN CHAUCER'S ENGLAND WERE KEPT BY THE Church and the Crown. Fair orchards, vineyards and groves of nut trees represented wealth in the days when self-sufficiency counted. In rich men's gardens there were stew ponds for fish and patches of hemp and flax for weaving into clothes, as well as pigs and a poultry yard. Herbs were grown for strewing in the house and to add variety to a dull diet. They were also used to cure all ills. The contemplation of these outdoor larders and medicine cupboards must have been a source of comfort and pride to their owners. Unlike the rest of the world, who toiled over ridge and furrow to earn a bare living, those higher up the social scale had time for leisure. They often chose to spend this out of doors (the climate was better then), in what has come to be thought of as a typical medieval garden. This was a small enclosure set apart from the business of growing your own livelihood, which was fenced or hedged from roaming animals and sheltered from winds. It had sanded paths, where a lady might walk up and down, through patches of 'flowery mead'. These were no more than rough lawns, where daisies, violets and often periwinkles were encouraged. Chaucer evokes this sort of garden in the *Knight's Tale* when the heroine, Emily, is pictured walking up and down, gathering flowers to make a May garland. Sometimes the plot would contain a rose bush at its centre, or water from a fountain or a well, but the simple layout did not often vary.

Opposite: In Cornish gardens like Glendurgan primroses still stud the grass in early spring as they must have done for the last 500 years. Before the days of weedkillers and fertilizers wild flowers like these grew everywhere. Ordinary people going about their lives saw flowers without needing to go near a garden and the majority of flowers grown in gardens were those which grew just as well, if a little smaller, in the wild.

In spring the park at Faringdon House in Oxfordshire looks like the ground in a medieval Paradise garden, but the tulips (apart from the yellow native Tulipa sylvestris*) would not have been known in England until the late sixteenth century when they were judged too rare for growing in grass. Tulips are difficult to naturalize but seem to do better when planted very deep. They prefer a sandy soil.*

When James I of Scotland gazed out of the window at Windsor, where he was kept captive around 1415, he described a garden which must have looked much the same for a hundred years and which would hardly change its character until the end of the sixteenth century.

> *Now was there made, fast by the towris wall*
> *A garden fair; and in the corners set*
> *An herbere green with wandis long and small*
> *Raillit about and so with treeis set*
> *Was all the place and Hawthorn hedges knet*
> *That lief was none warkyn therefore bye*
> *That might within scarce any wight espye.*

Enclosed gardens near the house, like the one he described, were private places, quite small with grass surrounded by railings, turf seats, a few flowers and often some water. After 1460 there might have been pots with carnations. This type of small garden, the *Hortus conclusus*, was in the tradition of the Mary Gardens which were made to celebrate the cult of the Virgin. In the favourite medieval image of Mary, she is painted serenely sitting

among her attendants in a small walled space apart from the world: the violets, lilies and daisies at her feet symbolize purity, the fruit in abundance represents fertility, and the roses flowering among their thorns suggest love and martyrdom. The Virgin was seen not as a saint on a pedestal, but as a mother or a beautiful woman in a garden. Her gardens, and those small plots dedicated to growing flowers for the Church and the Virgin, came to be known as Paradise Gardens. The medieval mind never strayed far from religion, and by association with these traditions and possibly those of the Old Testament, where the Garden of Eden was made to sound like Paradise, all gardens came to be thought of as places of heavenly happiness. 'Oh Paradise thy rival is this place', wrote an eleventh-century bishop. It is a simplification to say that all gardens up to the end of the sixteenth century were symbolic or spiritual, but that they were a means to an end, rather than an end in themselves seems almost certain to be true.

This allegorical tradition survived at the heart of gardening for four centuries. All that had belonged in the garden to the cult of the Virgin, the suggestion of Paradise and the treating of flowers as symbols of the cult figure, lingered on in pale imitation in the gardens of courtly love and was later adapted as a showplace for the power of Henry VIII and then for the glorification of Queen Elizabeth I. All flowers became sacred to the loved one: mistresses had their features compared with lilies, roses, violets, marigolds and pinks, as

Christopher Lloyd's flowery mead at Great Dixter in East Sussex is one of the most successful wild flower meadows in England. On clay soil where grass grows strongly buttercups do well and these are ancient native flora, but the camassias (or bear grass) would not have been seen in early gardens because these bulbs were only introduced from North America in 1827.

well as with primroses, cowslips, daisies and daffodils. Queen Elizabeth was personified as Flora and Spring, in an age when all flowers were spring flowers, before the introduction of plants from other continents which lengthened the flowering season into summer. The queen's clothes, unlike those of other Elizabethans who might wear the odd stylized flower, were strewn with the roses, pansies and pinks which became her own symbols, and, although she herself made no changes to her father's gardens, all over England gardens were made whose sole object was to receive and glorify the Virgin Queen.

It must have come more naturally to treat flowers as symbols at a time when they needed no coaxing to grow. Since the anti-bandit laws of 1285, it had been obligatory to clear a space 200 feet wide on either side of the roads between towns. Before the days of sprays and cutters, these verges must have looked like Botticelli's meadows. Ordinary people going about their lives saw flowers without needing to go near a garden and the majority of flowers grown in gardens were those which grew just as well, if a little smaller, in the wild. Gerard the herbalist was delighted to gather 'mallow, shepherd's purse, sweet woodruff, bugle, red clary, white saxifrage, sad-coloured rocket, yarrow, lesser hawkweed and trefoil' on an afternoon in Gray's Inn in 1596. If flowers grew so obligingly unaided, there was little point in bringing them into the garden unless they were either useful or significant; they were rarely cultivated for reasons of beauty alone. Our modern obsession with the way one plant looks with another played no part in gardening at all. For this

reason, although it is fascinating to see a collection of medieval plants like the one at the Cloisters Museum in New York, which was directly inspired by the Unicorn tapestries hanging in the museum, it is doubtful whether any early garden actually looked like this, since many of the flowers on the tapestries were part of the collective memory of the countryside, rather than from some particular garden.

The besetting sin of the Victorians may have been sentimentality, but in twentieth-century reconstruction work verisimilitude is clouded by the instinct of the collector and by modern ideas on taste. According to Dr John Harvey, who has done some invaluable research into early gardening catalogues, most sources suggest that the total number of plants in cultivation around 1400 did not greatly exceed a hundred, except in the unusual case of Friar Henry Daniel. The Cloisters Museum at the time of writing boasts over 200 plants, whose arrangement inevitably bears traces of twentieth-century leaf-scaping. Similarly, the garden at the Huntington Botanic Gardens in California dedicated to Shakespeare's flowers is thoroughly interesting from the point of view of seeing a collection of the flowers which Shakespeare wrote about, but is hardly an accurate picture of an Elizabethan garden.

All this might suggest that early gardeners had no love for flowers and were as happy to grow groundsel and chickweed for their medicines as they were to tend lilies and roses in honour of their religion, their queen, or their mistress. They certainly had an eye for the beauty of flowers, but it was tempered by different considerations from our own. The blooms of a Christmas rose by a cottage door might give pleasure through the winter months, but their real purpose was to ward off witches and evil spirits. Marigolds and mallows are examples of flowers which were grown as pot herbs; poppies, roses, knapweed, squills and clary were some of the ornamental plants whose purpose was primarily medicinal. If flowers were not doing duty as symbols, talismans or drugs, they were required, if nothing else, to fill the air with heavenly smells. Escaping from houses which in spite of strewn herbs, nosegays, pomanders and pot-pourri still probably smelt appalling, it must have been more refreshing to enjoy the air of the garden than to admire its flowers. The fact that many gardens were small and enclosed meant that the scent of roses, lilies and herbs hung perpetually in the still air, making a garden a more attractive place for dallying or plotting than the stuffy rooms indoors.

In small medieval and Tudor gardens the attitude to flowers was very different from our own; this was also the case in larger gardens. Cardinal Wolsey's work at Hampton

Court was on such a daring scale that in answer to the question 'Why should a subject build such a gorgeous palace?' he was forced to answer 'To give it to his master' for fear of losing his head. Gardens were seen as mirrors of their moving spirits and Henry VIII may have felt as much threatened by the garden as by the house. Yet, according to George Cavendish, Cardinal Wolsey's biographer, this garden was little more than the old *Hortus conclusus* writ large:

> My gardens sweet enclosed with walles strong
>> Embanked with benches to sytt and take my rest
> The knotts so enknotted it cannot be exprest
>> With arbors and allyes so pleasant and so dulce
> The pestylent ayres with flavors do repulse.

These lines of Cavendish's do not sound very different from James I of Scotland's description a hundred years earlier. After Henry had appropriated Hampton Court and Whitehall from Cardinal Wolsey and built himself the Palace of Nonsuch, he spent enormous sums of money on their gardens without adding much in the way of layout or plants that was new. It was more elaborate perhaps, and much grander in style than

Eleanor of Castile's crosses adorn England at the places where her coffin rested. She was a keen gardener and this monument in a garden dedicated to her at Winchester is a reminder of her thirteenth-century interest in fruit and flowers.

New College Mound in Oxford is now romantically overgrown, but it is still a good example of a late sixteenth-century mount. Modern mounts may not be needed for spying aliens over battlements, but can provide an interesting feature in a flat garden. Strategically placed, they will allow a view over fields beyond and act as a windbreak or a buffer between neighbours, who can then be looked down upon.

anything before, but the ingredients of the old medieval monastery and Paradise Gardens were still there: the walks, mounts, arbours, orchards, fountains, seats and knots that had been known in simpler forms for hundreds of years. What he did add were painted wooden posts at every turn, which were crowned with brightly coloured heraldic animals known as the King's Beasts. A simple Tudor rose was not enough to suggest Henry's larger-than-life-size majesty: dragons, greyhounds, lions and gryphons were gayer and more lasting reminders of the king than evanescent flowers.

Henry's mount at Hampton Court may have used thousands of bricks in its foundations and ended up larger than any other English mount, but it was essentially the same feature as that found in gardens all over the country. Mounts were originally no more than piles of earth thrown up against castle walls so that defenders might get a better view of their attackers and have the advantage of height when the time came to cast their slings and arrows at the enemy. After mounts ceased to be defensive, they continued to be enjoyed for the view they provided; the only way to see out of a garden enclosed by high walls or quick-set hedges was by climbing to the top of a mount. At Hampton Court the mount provided a view over the Thames on one side and down to the Privy Garden on the other. Mounts of less ambitious construction than Henry's lasted longer, and are still to be seen, such as the one at New College, Oxford, made in 1594, fifty years later.

Tudor mounts had another purpose besides giving a view over castle or garden walls: they were the right height for looking down on the increasingly complicated pattern of flower beds which dominated sixteenth-century garden design. It seems likely that knot gardens and mazes were both influenced by the elaborate patterns traced on church floors in the Middle Ages. These were designed as part of a ritual for penitents, who would shuffle through the twists of pattern on their knees, stopping to pray at various points, until they emerged at the altar and received absolution at the other end. A modern version of a religious maze exists at Grey's Court, near Reading, which was opened by the Archbishop of Canterbury in 1981. Like this twentieth-century example, early mazes were not generally designed to lose people behind high hedges. According to one contemporary writer, the hedges around the labyrinth at Nonsuch were so high that one could not see over them, but this was unusual and is generally a feature of later gardens where yew rather than box was used. Labyrinths or mazes may also have been an easy way of taking exercise in a small space. It might take a good twenty minutes to negotiate a turf maze laid out over an area small enough to be walked in under five.

As labyrinthine patterns curled over the clothes and furniture of the period, it is not surprising that they were also to be found in the garden. The division of flower gardens into squares and rectangles had gone on throughout the fourteenth and fifteenth centuries,

At Cranborne Manor in Dorset a gentle rise in the ground is made to seem higher and more like an ancient mount by the addition of clipped yew bushes. Solid evergreen shapes are the best ageing device for any garden and yew is not as slow as most people believe. With care and constant feeding it will grow a foot a year, but unlike other fast growing hedging plants it only needs one annual cut.

Above: The painted railings, herbs and sanded walks at Southampton University's Tudor Garden perfectly capture the spirit of an early garden. Dry walks amidst the scent of lavender could be enjoyed and from a shaded seat the garden was surveyed. (The double yellow Flore pleno *is a form of the wild buttercup. It was a favourite Elizabethan flower and is easy to grow in sun, but it likes a little moisture.)*

Left: Among the herbs grown at Southampton's Tudor garden is rosemary, which was introduced as early as 1388 by Queen Philippa, who had a parcel of cuttings from Europe. Instructions for sending this plant long distances survive in a French housekeeping manual written in 1393, which reveals that if the branches are wrapped in waxed cloth, sealed and smeared with honey all over and then powdered with flour they can be sent anywhere. They must have made very unattractive parcels for medieval messengers. Rosemary needs to be clipped annually after flowering if it is not to get woody.

At Helmingham Hall in Suffolk a recently executed knot garden looks convincingly early beside the moat. This is not something to attempt where labour is in short supply. Box hedges need to be immaculately kept if the design is to stay as crisp as this. The dwarf box for edging knot gardens is Buxus 'Suffruticosa', which can be clipped to only a few inches high. Other forms will need more cutting and be harder to control.

when it is likely that each type of plant would have been grown separately. Pansies, roses, lilies, primroses and columbines, as well as periwinkles, poppies, marigolds and lupins are some of the flowers which might have been found growing in this way, along with a few herbs in a small garden where there was not enough room for a separate herb garden. Until almost the end of the sixteenth century most of the flowers which were available would have been over by July, barring poppies, hollyhocks, monkshoods and a few roses, according to Francis Bacon. These hardly made for colour in the flower beds as we know it today, but as grand gardens were increasingly arranged to be seen from the state apartments on the first floor, coloured earth was occasionally found to serve as well as and better than flowers or herbs for showing off the increasingly elaborate layout of the beds. Knot gardens which relied on pattern for their effect were so popular that Bacon appeared to be heartily sick of them complaining 'that you may see as good sights as many times in tarts'.

It was also true that as the divisions were made smaller and more intricate, less space was available for flowers which were anyway not up to the demands of the design and continued to look better in the wild. After 1500 the edging plants for these knot gardens were most frequently herbs; hyssop, thyme, thrift and rosemary are all recorded. Dwarf box was not introduced until 1595. Santolina, or cotton lavender, is often mentioned nowadays as a plant used in knot gardens and, although it does appear in William Turner's herbal dedicated to Queen Elizabeth in 1568, John Parkinson, the king's botanist, was still writing of santolina as 'rare and novel' in 1629, so it seems unlikely that it was planted in any great quantities. On the Continent, germander was often used and, although there is no record of it here, it may well have been used as an edging plant.

A herb garden and a box labyrinth have recently been made at Hatfield in front of the Old Palace. This building, which dates from around 1490, belonged to Henry VIII, who used it as a nursery for his children. During her sister's reign Elizabeth was held at Hatfield. The thought that she must often have walked to and fro in a garden belonging to the Old Palace inspired this reconstruction. Many of the flowers now used at Hatfield were known to have been grown in the fifteenth and sixteenth centuries, and there are also plants from the early part of the seventeenth century, but their arrangement may be too pretty to be convincing. It is likely that the Tudor knot garden had less in common with the style of Sissinghurst Decorative than with that of Municipal Geometric.

Like the flowers, the trees were also carefully arranged in artificial curves or lines, and they were there for the purpose of giving shade, rather than to be admired as single specimens. Many of them were trained to form alleys or tunnels, where shady walks might be taken. At Little Haseley in Oxfordshire, a tunnel of hornbeam trained over iron hoops gives a feeling of being in an early garden, although the arbour in a medieval garden would have been supported not by iron but by wood; light poles of coppicings from hazel or willow were the most usual for carpentry. In some of the great gardens it was possible to walk out of the sun for as long as an hour; at Theobalds in Hertfordshire, which belonged to Lord Burleigh, there were over two miles of covered walks and arbours.

Pleaching and training trees into alleys was not the only way of treating trees as artificial objects. Tortured topiary, which Pliny is said to have practised and certainly wrote about, was everywhere in Tudor gardens. Like the hedges which made the labyrinths, topiary was most frequently cut out of box. In *Twelfth Night*, Sir Andrew Aguecheek and his two friends are all able to hide from Malvolio inside one box tree and, since it is unlikely that an untended box bush would have been seen in 1600, Shakespeare must have been thinking of some large topiarized bush in a garden familiar to him. Yew was not used much in gardens until the seventeenth century, when the diarist John Evelyn encouraged the planting of this native tree. There are known to have been works of topiary at Little Haseley, as there are now, and it is possible that the original box chessmen were replaced in

At Haseley Court in Oxfordshire a tunnel arbour of beech is trained over iron hoops. Early arbours were trained on wooden frames, generally made of hazel or willow. The light at the end of the tunnel is provided by patches of wallflowers which also scent the air around the well placed seat.

This avenue of limes at Mottisfont in Hampshire provides the sort of shady walk that was always popular when pale complexions were prized. Limes for avenues need to be grown from the same clone of the common lime, or they will vary in size and shape. Some clones tend to sprout at the base, which will ultimately weaken the tree. Limes propagated in Holland, which are nearer in habit to Tilia cordata than Tilia platyphyllos, are safest if the hybrid form (Tilia x europaea) is used.

At Cranborne Manor well-grown espaliers of apples are in a very old tradition. Trained fruit trees are not hard to manage once the shape is established. Summer pruning reduces the side shoots to a short distance from the main stem and with a light pruning again in winter this is all the attention they need.

the early nineteenth century, as they were said to have been at Chastleton in Oxfordshire. Some of the figures now in the garden, which are made of Portugal laurel and yew, are unlikely to have been part of the earlier garden.

Henry's topiary at Hampton Court was anyway not made of box, but of hawthorn or rosemary, tied and trained with willow into shapes of animals or men and women. It was in Henry's character to demand quick growing shrubs for maximum effect, rather than wait years for box to mature. He may have visited the Earl of Northumberland's castle at Wressle in Yorkshire, where topiary had been introduced early in the sixteenth century. This was thought to have been one of the first examples of the art in England. If this is true, it would have been well established by 1534, when Henry started showing off out of doors. Topiary at Hampton Court and Nonsuch was yet another way of treating plants as adjuncts of Henry's personality. It was designed to amaze and amuse as much as the heraldic beasts or the regally patterned flower beds. Today the fox and hounds cut out of yew at Longleat are nearer to the spirit of sixteenth-century topiary than the romantic bulges of Levens Hall in Cumbria.

Fruit trees were also trained; they were used for espalier work, and were extremely popular for walks and bowers. They attracted far more attention in Tudor gardens than they do today. Blossoming fruit trees must have made a decorative as well as

an edible contribution in gardens where flowers were not a particularly conspicuous feature. While flowers were being played down, fruit growing was on the up and up. In the Hampton Court accounts, the only flowers mentioned are roses, but the king spent large sums of money on fruit trees and repeatedly sent his gardener to France in search of new varieties. The pippin and the apricot were both brought back to England around 1542 to please him, and by the middle of the sixteenth century, fruit growing had become a craze. Any self-respecting gardener would have included 'pear, wardens and apples of diverse sorts'; also 'cherry, filberdes, bulleys, dampsons plummes, walnuttes and such other in his orchard'. John Parkinson listed fifty-four varieties of apple, and even Shakespeare acknowledged the obsession with fruit growing when he made Justice Shallow invite Falstaff, not to see his garden and some rare new flower as we might today, but 'to see mine orchard, where in an arbour we will eat a last year's pippin of my own grafting'. Alleys of pleached apples and pears were made to walk through and we know that vines were trained over hoops to make shady tunnels. Vines seem to have gone out of fashion when their culture went into a gradual decline after about 1350, as the course of the Gulf Stream changed and English summers became cooler and shorter. It is possible, too, that grapes were less expertly grown after the dissolution of the monasteries, when there were fewer monks around to pass on the techniques of cultivation.

Heartsease and foxgloves are no longer used as herbal remedies. Like many other plants which are now only grown for their ornamental value, these flowers once owed their place in the garden to their medicinal qualities. Dr Johnson suggested that the name pansy was derived from panacea, 'for it is known to be an excellent cure for the French pox'.

Beneath the arbours seats were placed. At their most sophisticated, these were banked up turves with a brick surround; the cruder sorts might have had wooden posts or wattle hurdles to retain the earth. Modern examples of these can be seen at Sissinghurst in Kent and at Hatfield, where sweet-smelling herbs like pennyroyal or thyme have been planted on top of the seats as they occasionally were in Henry's and Elizabeth's time. Similarly, the earth around the roots of trees was often heaped up and surrounded with wattle or stone to make a seat, as it is in the painting by Sir Isaac Oliver of a melancholy young man resting under a tree.

Tudor gardens were not only used as places in which to stroll in the shade or sit, they were also dedicated to games. At Hampton Court, archery and tennis were both enjoyed by Henry, who was one of the best archers in the kingdom and no mean tennis player until his later ruined years. In addition, there would have been fine lawns for bowling, as there were in gardens all over England. Bowling always used to be played in the side alleys belonging to taverns in the fourteenth and fifteenth centuries. 'A bowl alley is the place where there are three things thrown away besides bowls, to wit, time, money and curses,' wrote a contemporary author. In 1541 Henry's government passed an act fining anyone who played the game of bowls outside his own garden or orchard; this was for two reasons: to discourage gambling and drunkenness and to give archery pride of place as a game of skill, which was still considered important from a military point of view. It was, after all, only twenty-eight years since James IV of Scotland had been defeated by bows at Flodden and, although Tudor firearms existed, Henry was anxious to maintain the traditions of English archery for his infantry. The law did little to slow down the decline of the bow and arrow, but it did wonders for the tradition of the English lawn.

After Henry's death, the standard of living rose rapidly. Bacon wrote of England that Elizabeth had 'received it a realm of cottages and made it a realm of palaces'. All over the land, manor houses were built and enlarged, often from the ruins of the plundered abbeys, and people had time and money to enjoy life as never before. Gardening books began to appear which were mostly translations of foreign works, but the fact that they did appear indicates that ordinary people as well as nobles were now showing an interest in plants and gardens which in turn created a popular demand for books like Thomas Hill's (or Didymus Mountain's) *Gardener's Labyrinth* or Thomas Tusser's *A Hundred Good Points of Husbandry,* (which was later expanded to *Five Hundred*). Tusser does not suggest much that departs from the flowers grown in earlier gardens and the book is on a strictly practical level; when to sow seeds, what kind of manure is best, or how to weed are the topics on which he dwells, in moral and rather priggish rhymes. Mountain, who is usually credited with the earliest serious gardening book in English, written in 1558 and still in circulation fifty years later, did not produce an original work, but a hotch-potch of translated tips, taken mostly from gardeners who gardened in warmer climates than our own.

Although gardening lore was in its infancy in Elizabeth's reign, there is no doubt that horticulture was increasingly fashionable and curious plants arrived back in quantities from the newly discovered corners of the earth to satisfy the current interest throughout the latter half of the sixteenth century. Marigolds from Mexico, potatoes from South America, the Damask rose from Persia, auriculas from The Alps and many other plants all came home to Elizabethan England to be written up in the new herbals of Messrs Turner and Gerard. As horticultural finds became more widely available, gardening was enjoyed by more people. Squires like Sir Henry Fanshawe employed 'a delicate and diligent curiosity' about their plants. 'He did', wrote Sir Henry Wotton, 'so precisely examine the

Opposite: This box tree at Cranborne Manor must be about the same size as the one which Shakespeare describes in Twelfth Night, *where Sir Andrew Aguecheek and his friends hid from Malvolio. Box is very slow indeed. Yew would make a quicker hiding place, or an arbour, in about a third of the time it would take box to reach the same size.*

Little Moreton Hall in Cheshire perfectly illustrates Samuel Pepys' description of plain English gardens dedicated to the business of Ayre where 'we have the best walks of gravell in the world'.

tinctures and seasons of his flowres that in their setting the inwardest of those which were to come up at the same time, should always be a little darker than the outmost and to serve them for a kinde of gentle shadow, like a piece not of Nature but of Arte.' Rich men on the whole were content to garden as their ancestors had done, without much thought of art. They were slow to realize the possibilities of gardening as a display of wealth and importance. They excelled at showing off in bricks and mortar, but only rarely did it occur to them to link the garden to the design of the house. We know of the eccentric Nottinghamshire landowner Sir Francis Willoughby who planned his house and garden as an entity, but he was an exception. Gardens were not planned axially, but fitted into the scraps of land around the all-important building. 'A man shall ever see that when ages grow to civility and elegancy, men come to build stately sooner than to garden finely', wrote Bacon, and even Lord Burleigh's plans for Theobalds, which was among the largest and most famous of Elizabethan gardens, appear on paper as restless scribbles, where nothing is aligned and the proportions are thoroughly dismaying.

Gardening was slow to become an art. It was not until Anne of Denmark, James I's wife, discovered and employed the brilliant Huguenot Solomon de Caus in the early years of the seventeenth century that the English upper classes realized the possibilities of architecture out of doors. Looking back on the turn of the century, around 1660, John

Aubrey was to write: 'The pleasure and use of gardens were unknown to our great grandfathers: they were contented with pot-herbs and did mind chiefly their stables.' Bacon's famous essay, *Of Gardens*, tells us not so much what a garden was actually like at the turn of the century, but rather that gardening was a subject which the intelligent man would do well to contemplate. His essay is a plea for a carefully thought out princely garden, where he has 'spared no cost'. Bacon set the seal on the intellectual respectability of gardening. It was no longer to be the province of princes, monks or farmers' wives; it was to be an art fit for Renaissance man.

The simplest knot gardens like this one at Helmingham Hall were, according to the herbalist Parkinson, suitable for outlandish flowers. Their compartments of evergreen make a good background for specimen plants, but today they are more often filled with permanent or bedding plants of one variety, as they are here.

CHAPTER 2

AVENUES, GROVES, GROTTOS & CANALS

'Tis all enforced the fountain and the grot'

Llannerch, Denbighshire. *British School (c. 1662–72)*

CHARLES I WAS A CULTIVATED MAN AND HIS SAD REIGN WAS
one of great architectural distinction. The tone for matters of taste was set
by the court during most of the seventeenth century. Inigo Jones was employed
by the king as surveyor of royal buildings; under his influence Palladianism and
all things Italianate spread far outside the capital, reinforcing Renaissance ideals.
Classics still had the monopoly of attention at the universities and educated men
were familiar with classical texts and works on antiquities. Architecture and craftsmanship
were favourite topics in an age when most pictures were portraits.

It was not surprising that gardens should reflect these interests, as they were later to
reflect the eighteenth-century preoccupation with painting. Straight lines extended from
the house into the garden. Axial dominance had come to stay. Statues were *de rigueur*.
Inigo Jones made a garden for Lord Arundel which was a showplace for the Arundel
collection of classical statues. His theatrical drawings for court masques included pavilions
and grottos inspired by Italian models which he had sketched on his travels. Other scenes
showed tree-lined vistas, gateways or grottos, and these miniature landscapes were soon
enlarged and copied in real gardens beyond the world of the court masque and London.
Travellers, like John Evelyn, made Italianate gardens with terraces and descending double
staircases, like the ones they had seen abroad. Grottos and fountains began to appear in

*Opposite: Although William and Mary spent plenty
of money on their own gardens, Dutch gardens
never really caught on in England. Westbury Court
in Gloucestershire is an unusual example of the
Dutch style, with water and simple flower beds
filled with florists' flowers. Its owner Maynard
Colchester had a Dutch neighbour with whom he
was friendly. This may account for the horticultural
emphasis and the 'nookiness' of the garden, which
is more Dutch in character than French.*

The garden at Powis Castle in Wales is an unusual survival. Its hanging terraces with their lead statues escaped landscaping in the eighteenth century and now provide a series of terraces where rare and tender plants thrive.

Dutch gardens, like the one at Westbury Court, always had plenty of pots, which are a time-consuming adornment but well worth the trouble. They can provide an architectural element in today's small gardens and modern composts and water-retaining granules make their management less difficult than it used to be.

strange places. A Mr Povey in Lincoln's Inn Fields had a grotto in the basement of his house and an eccentric former servant of Francis Bacon spent £10,000 on a hermitage and grotto formed from natural rocks in Oxfordshire. Charles I and Henrietta Maria visited the hermit of Enstone in 1635 and were treated to a display of special effects, which included rainbows accompanied by the sounds of nightingales and drums. At Wilton, the Earl of Pembroke laid out a princely garden whose design was based on that of a Venetian villa. Inigo Jones supervised the work here, with Isaac de Caus, (brother of Solomon) imposing a unity and order on the landscape which was unequalled in grandeur anywhere in England.

If the influence of Italian architecture emanated strongly from the court, so too did French ideas of what was proper out of doors. The king's wife, Henrietta Maria, was sister to the king of France. She employed a French gardener, André Mollet, one of a family of gardeners, to remake the gardens at Wimbledon Manor. There, rectangular knot gardens were cleared to make curling panels of French embroidered parterres or cut turf, while hedged groves and a maze replaced the traditional orchards. Mollet and his brother were greatly sought after as designers, and they stayed on in England during the Commonwealth. However, I do not think the English ever felt happy in French gardens. The Mollets gave a French gloss to many English landscapes, which was never more than superficial. This is often attributed to Le Nôtre who in fact never came to England.

Order and display were twin gods of the French style. The Mollets and those who copied them liked their gardens to look as large and as perfect as possible. Miles of avenues were designed to make houses look imposing and the preferred French layout was long and thin, to accommodate these daunting perspectives. Avenues marched out from the house as far as the eye could see, while the contrived and sterile parterres in front of the building provided few flowers. The Mollets are credited with one introduction which did suit the English landscape. They used a system of five avenues radiating out from a semi-circle (known as *patte d'oie* or goose foot) which Le Nôtre always included in his gardens in France, but with a difference. Le Nôtre used the device in the park as a view-point for his hunting-mad clients. The Mollets tied it to a vista from the house, so that five alleys beckoned the walker and when he had walked the length of the avenue and turned across the wedge of woodland at the top, there would be a different view back to the house. If he cared to walk further, the angle of vision would shift again. In England, because of the later landscape movement, few of these *pattes d'oie* now remain. At Bramham in Yorkshire an example on a grand scale was replanted after gale damage in 1962. At Inkpen House, in Berkshire, the same arrangement also exists, but cutting back and replanting has recently taken place there because of over-maturity. The best mature example of the kind of effect that the Mollets wanted to create is at St Paul's Walden Bury.

Creating a fashionable garden in the seventeenth century was not something to be undertaken if you were short of money. The expense on canals, ironwork, statues and fountains was prodigious but plenty of people engaged craftsmen to do work which is now lost. These iron gates at Melbourne Hall in Derbyshire would have been fine in their day, but not unique as they are now.

Above: At Kingston Lacy in Dorset a fine lime avenue forms a tunnel to the light. This is not an effect which can be realized in many gardens, but something along similar lines can be created with a walk of arching hazel nuts or Philadelphus 'Virginal'.

Opposite: Like the limes at Kingston Lacy, these beeches at Oare House in Wiltshire make a feature on the grand scale. But their underplanting is not impossible. An avenue of cow parsley is an effect which never fails to please.

After the Restoration there was still a Mollet on hand to advise on the Royal Gardens. It was as though there had never been a Civil War. Charles II landed at Dover at the end of May 1660. By September of that year the latest in garden devices was being created in St James's Park. A straight sheet of water was spread below the steps of Whitehall Palace. In the following year an even larger expanse of water was laid out in front of Hampton Court. This was designed in honour of Charles's bride, the plain but rich Catherine of Braganza. She must have been impressed by her newly gilded balcony with a view of the vast canal flanked by 758 lime trees in orderly array. It was not long before these flat surfaces of water started to appear in lesser gardens.

Creating a fashionable garden in the second half of the seventeenth century was not something to be undertaken if you were short of money. The expense of canals, ironwork, lead statues, carpentry, fountains and plants was enormous. At Longleat, for example, improvements in the 1680s cost £30,000, which was a considerable sum in those days. Moreover, organizing the craftsmen and plants to embellish these gardens was not a task for the amateur. A professional soon emerged to take charge of the proceedings. George London had acquired a taste for rare plants when working for the bishop of London. He joined a partnership which founded a nursery garden in Brompton Park in 1681. There was money to be made in supplying trees for groves and 'greens' (evergreens) for parterres.

The parterre at Cliveden in Buckinghamshire is breathtaking. Its scale would have delighted the gardeners of the seventeenth century who liked to put their stamp on the horizon, but its execution was originally Victorian and has since been simplified. However, the Duke of Buckingham, who built Cliveden after the Restoration, did have a parterre which John Evelyn described 'as a circular view to the utmost verge of the horizon'.

41

Top: This wrought iron arbour by Robert Bakewell was made for Melbourne Hall in Derbyshire in 1706.

Bottom: The view of sky through Bakewell's leafy ironwork is so beautiful that creepers and roses would spoil it. Wirework arbours, which were a later invention, are often reproduced today. Their similar, but lighter, effect is also best left unembellished.

Opposite: The sea horse fountain at Chatsworth in Derbyshire was carved by Cibber. Under English skies fountains can look less inspiring than they do in warmer countries, but when the sun shines they are a dazzling feature.

There was also a market for advising on and supervising improvements. London became a garden consultant and designer, who was very much in demand all over England. He worked with Talman the architect, Tijou the ironworker and Van Nost the sculptor, and he established such a name for himself that he was appointed Royal Gardener to William and Mary, whose interests in gardening and architecture had been demonstrated in Holland at Het Loo, before they came to England. This couple spent lavishly on their English gardens in the first four years of their reign, and most of this was on Hampton Court, where London was in charge.

The point of a French garden was to show off, but in England people were less keen on display. It is in the English character to show less enthusiasm about display. Unlike the French, the English have always been good at living in the country. Noblesse has traditionally obliged by providing employment, dispensing law and attending to agriculture. The possessor of such a defined role may not have felt the need to aggrandize himself if his social position locally was unquestionable. Later in the century, the Duke of Montagu, returning from his embassy at Versailles, talked of planting an avenue to run all the way from Boughton in Northamptonshire to London, a distance of seventy miles.

On the whole, however, the French influence appeared in a very diluted form. By the time it reached the shires, the scale and the smartness seem to have dwindled. What remained were the straight lines and the avenues. Often the parterres were abandoned (they were difficult to maintain), so that in many paintings of the period, gardens in front of country houses have four grass plats, perhaps with a simple fountain where the paths cross. These puritanical versions of flamboyant arrangements found across the Channel were called *parterres Anglaises*. Here the use of 'Anglaise' has the same effect as it does in '*crème Anglaise*'. Custard is impoverished cream; *parterres Anglaises* were impoverished flower gardens. But these immaculate lawns came to be a source of envy for the French, who although not much given to the art of understatement could acknowledge success when they saw it. Sometimes there were statues set in the centre of each plat. At Ham House, in Surrey, in a painting by Danckwerts, statues lined the edges of the wilderness and well-kept grass was laid out before the house. Good lawns, without the aid of mowing machines or automatic sprinklers, needed many hours of labour to keep them green. As a status symbol the hand-cut lawn must have rated high, and our temperate climate has always ensured that in this feature of the garden we have no rival. Samuel Pepys summed up the played-down philosophy of some English gardens in 1666 with the following words:

> Of the present fashion of gardens to make them plain, that we have the best walks of gravell in the world, France having none nor Italy and our green of our bowling alleys is better than any they have. So our business here being Ayre, this is the best way, only with a little mixture of statues or pots which may be handsome and so filled with another pot of such or such a flower of green as the season will bear. And then for flowers, they are best seen in a little plot by themselves.

The key to this is of course the matter of 'Ayre'. The French used their gardens for sitting and socializing; the English, because of the weather, have always needed to keep on the move. Gravel or mown grass underfoot, with enough space to walk, were the most important features in a garden before the days of footpaths and way marks, while nature was still beyond the pale.

The cult of display and ownership was an important element in some particularly

An inspired reconstruction of a seventeenth-century knot garden has been made in the garden of the deconsecrated Church of St Mary at Lambeth. Tradescant was buried here and the garden is a memorial to two generations of this family of gardeners and plant collectors. The grey-leaved santolina often formed clipped compartments in early gardens. It is easy to grow in sun and well-drained soil but can disappear in very cold winters, so it is important to keep some reserve cuttings in a sheltered place. Like lavender, santolina should not be clipped until after the worst of the weather is over.

aristocratic gardens before the eighteenth-century landscape movement. Networks of avenues invaded the countryside as far as the eye could see around places like Badminton or Chatsworth. Those who were less keen to parade the extent of their property found other ways of making their mark, by displaying their culture. Scientific knowledge was increasingly fashionable. Amateur botanists and collectors were numerous and their academic interest in the curious and the novel was insatiable. The first Earl of Salisbury even had a professional plant collector, John Tradescant, whose travels he financed to find new plants. Tradescant brought back fruit trees and flowers from Holland and France to plant at Hatfield, where he was regarded as something more than a gardener. Another rich patron, the Duke of Buckingham, enabled him to go to Africa and yet another, Sir Dudley Digges, took him to Russia. He also owned a small share in a Virginian colony, which gave him first pick of the plants from the New World, like *Tradescantia virginiana* (spiderwort) which was named after him. Tradescant was finally able to set up a place of his own in Lambeth, where he founded a nursery and a museum of the curiosities which he had acquired during a lifetime of travel. When he died, his business and his appointment as Royal Gardener at Oatlands, in Surrey, passed to his son, who carried on his father's tradition of collecting and providing information about plants.

Inspired no doubt by the Tradescant example, and by the current interest in

plants, the first botanic garden in England was in its preliminary stages in 1621. At Oxford, the Earl of Danby allocated five acres near Magdalen College for the purpose of establishing a botanic garden. In 1637 John Tradescant's help was enlisted, to supervise and supply plants for the garden, but he died the following year. The Oxford Physic Garden was surrounded by fourteen-foot-high walls, which enclosed the collection of plants, and the beds were laid out in rows in quarter plots. One quarter was reserved for each of the four continents of the world. Physic herbs had first call on the garden, which was attached to the medical school of the University. The study of herbs was a discipline to encourage in the days before country doctors existed. Every manor house and hall grew a collection of 'simples' or herbs which could be used as cure-alls for commonplace ills. The research at the botanic garden promised well for increasing that stock of home-grown remedies. Jacob Bobart, the German who was put in charge of the garden, had a collection of over 1600 plants by 1648. Over the next ten years another 400 were added, and out of all these only 600 were plants from England. A hundred years later this enthusiasm for collecting had added another 1500 plants to the gardener's palette. This is a huge increase from the 100 plants in general cultivation at the beginning of the fifteenth century.

Meanwhile, private gardeners were also collecting. Sir Thomas Hanmer lived in Wales at Bettisfield. He was married to one of the queen's maids of honour and had been

The large knot garden in front of the Old Palace at Hatfield is also a reconstruction, using only plants of the period. Day lilies, sweet rocket, the magenta Gladiolus byzantinus *and old roses grow in sweet disarray among herbs and curlicues of box.*

Above: Eremurus, or foxtail lilies, have the same towering, out-of-scale effect as topiary in a flowerbed. Other giant plants for a surprising change of scale are the great grey thistle (Onopordum), or the flowering giant kale (Crambe cordifolia). Eremurus were introduced by the Victorians, who brought back topiary to the English garden.

This simple pattern of box hedges laid out at Cranborne Manor in Dorset covers only a small piece of ground. It is filled with an informal mixture of flowers and herbs and might be adapted for use in gardens where space is short. A collection of bright alpines for spring could be grown in box diagonals. Hedges improve drainage by taking moisture out of the ground, so they have a practical as well as an ornamental use.

The topiary work at Levens Hall in Cumbria is much larger than it was meant to be in the seventeenth century, when it was first planted. The mysterious bulky shapes make this garden a thrilling place even on a rainy day. Topiary is vegetable sculpture and will provide a focal point in any garden. The trick is to follow the shape of the bush. If it looks like a chicken it will never make a peacock.

close to the king. When Cromwell came to power, he slipped away from London to live quietly on his estate, where he produced the *Garden Book of Sir Thomas Hanmer* in 1659. This work is full of information on what a garden of that date comprised. Large gardens were 'commonly a third part longer than broad and cannot well be less than two or three hundred yards in length', although smaller gardens were made in a rectangle about 70 feet long. He describes the new open garden with vistas and more space near the house ('laid open and exposed to the sight of the rooms and chambers'). In large gardens, beyond this space were found parterres in the French, or Dutch, manner, with low-growing flowers. Topiary and statues set in grass, groves for birds with gravel walks between and fountains and cascades also featured. Sir Thomas's heart was not really in design or display. What interested him was 'the little private seminary to keep such treasures as are not to be exposed to everyone's view and a winter home for the shelter of plants'.

Hanmer and his friend John Rea were passionate collectors. In 1656 he was watching with delight a two-foot stalk brought back from the West Indies 'on top whereof came two flowers shaped like lilies, of a fine shining red colour betwixt an orange and a pink'. It is hard for us to understand the exotic romance of growing an unknown flower from the other side of the world. We buy our amaryllis packaged for presents in the supermarket. Sir Thomas Hanmer's bulb was a mystery to him until it flowered. He also grew 52

Above: Like a strange golden mollusc, the Levens spiral of yew leans over the forget-me-nots.

Left: The leaning corkscrew of Levens would not have been easy to achieve. Dutch nurseries produce trained specimens which are wired for shape and which can be bought and trained on, but amateurs would need a steady hand and a good eye to grow a golden yew like this one.

kinds of tulip. (He was described by his friend Rea as 'an ingenious lover of these rarities'.) The best of these was named after him: 'Agate Hanmer, a beautiful flower of three good colours, pale grideline [purple], deep scarlet and pure white, commonly well parted, striped, agated and excellently placed, abiding constant to the last with the bottom and stamens blue.' He also grew crown imperials, iris raised from seed, polyanthemums, daffodils, anemones, jonquils, hyacinths, fritillaries and colchicums, all in the four little bordered beds where he housed his tulip collection. His garden must have looked like a smaller version of the botanic garden.

Lower down the social scale a different sort of plant collecting had caught on. Florists' societies were started by Huguenot weavers who specialized in breeding certain sorts of flowers. They concentrated on the differences in detail between varieties and competed with each other to perfect new forms. Later, this obsessional hobby was taken up by cottage craftsmen all over England. Artisans who worked at home were well placed for tending showy and temperamental flowers like auriculas, tulips and pinks. If it rained they could hurry out from their looms to move the plants indoors. If the sun became too hot, they could leave their work to shade them. They concocted disgusting potions of manure or 'green slime of still water mixed with fresh earth' on which they fed their beauties, and when show days came, they trudged twenty miles with potted plants in buckets dangling

from a yoke on their backs. The flowers which the florists grew had narrowed to only eight varieties by the end of the eighteenth century, but in the early days of the florists' societies around the middle of the seventeenth century the range was larger. The tulip was particularly popular. Tulipomania reached its height in the 1630s, when bulbs of these plants sold like futures in the stock market today. Some bulb fanciers went bankrupt gambling on the fashion for these flowers, whose highly bred variations have not survived in the absence of such horticultural dedication.

In the seventeenth century gardens still had spiritual connotations which no longer exist today. References to classical learning and the Bible outside the house demonstrated what scholarship and learning went on inside. The Paradise Garden was not a dominant symbolic theme as it had been in the Middle Ages, but thoughts of gardens often came paired with thoughts of Eden (or Arcadia for the more classically inclined). It was an age pre-occupied with original sin, the fall of man and the loss of Paradise, and the garden was a part of that mythology. Contemporary thinking held that the making of a garden was divine. John Parkinson, (who wrote a book which listed 1000 plants in cultivation in England), described creating an earthly Paradise as though it were an act of worship. Puritans believed in the dignity of manual labour; gardens were moral places. William Prynne, the Puritan pamphleteer, wrote that: 'If Bibles fail, each garden will descry the works of God to us.' The knowledge of God which had been lost at the expense of gaining the knowledge of the world could be redeemed in a garden. John Evelyn, in his *Kalendarium*, wrote that gardens should be made 'as near as we can contrive them to the garden of Eden', and talked about kings and philosophers 'who when they would frame a type of Heaven, describe a garden and call it Elysium'.

More particularly, orchards were also designated sacred places. Ralph Austen, a Calvinist proctor of Oxford University, wrote a treatise on fruit trees which included a section on the 'Spiritual use of an Orchard: held forth in diverse Similitudes between Naturall and Spirituall Fruit trees: according to Scripture and Experience'. In this work, God was described as the 'great Husband man of His orchard'. Austen was not alone in regarding fruit as the ultimate symbol of goodness. 'I gather flowers (my fruits are only flowers),' wrote the poet Marvell, using this poignant metaphor to describe the human acts that he offered up to God as an oblation. Growing fruit was more than a civilized pastime for country gentlemen; it also had overtones of virtue and divine blessing.

The new formality appealed to these spiritual gardeners, for had not God created order out of chaos? (Sir Thomas Browne even believed that the trees in Paradise were planted in rows.) Avenues were instantly popular because they imposed order on the chaos of nature, while the so-called 'wildernesses' in gardens were very far from wild. They often consisted of diagonal rows of trees, planted quincunx-form, in the shape of a diamond with a point at its centre and surrounded by neat hedges. This quincunx formation had mystic properties. The figure five is made up of the first even, and the first odd, numbers and represents God the unity, combined with diversity, i.e. the sum of creation. Trees were evenly spaced at fifteen feet apart and between these geometric plantations were closely mown walks. A good example of such a wilderness can be seen at Ham House. This was replanted to a contemporary plan eight years ago, which means that it looks now much as it would

Opposite: The alliums at Cranborne Manor in Dorset are in a very old tradition. Garlic was grown in many varieties in the sixteenth and seventeenth centuries. 'They will grow in any soil, the flowers being fit for nothing, but to set with others in pots,' wrote one disdainful florist. Alliums are easy if given sun, and the ornamental varieties do not smell of garlic unless crushed. But the wild white allium will scent the air for miles around and is very invasive.

have looked in its infancy 300 years ago. Nature was subdued by artifice at every turn. No wonder some people, like Marvell, thought it had all gone too far:

> *Tis all enforced the fountain and the grot*
> *While the sweet fields do lie forgot*
> *Where willing Nature does to all dispense*
> *A wild and fragrant innocence.*

Gardens, with all their religious and classical associations, were part of the intellectual life of the day. Thoughts of eternal spring haunted the minds of civilized men and at this time certainly had some influence on their garden making. This medieval theme had its sources in the Bible and the classics. In the Garden of Eden there had been no seasons; fruit and flowers appeared simultaneously. In Ovid's golden age the earth produced its crops without being cultivated by man and in the Arcadia of the pastoral poets it was always spring. Legends of spring (with a flavour of harvest festival) must have seemed very appealing in the days of colder, darker winters, when houses could not be lit or warmed at the touch of a switch, as they can nowadays. Prolonging the flowering season was something that was much discussed.

Beech hedges like these, which have been restored since they were first planted around 1730, are very quick to mature. Beech can be planted at 5 to 6 feet high and will make an imposing hedge within three to four years. In ten years it will look as though it has been planted for fifty, but it only needs cutting once a year, which can be done in winter.

Opposite: The patte d'oie at St Paul's Walden Bury in Hertfordshire is a charming English version of a French device. Behind clipped hedges are groves of overgrown trees, which would in the seventeenth century have been severely trimmed.

53

This plane tree at Christ Church in Oxford was planted in 1636, by Edward Pococke who brought it back from the East.

Bacon, in an essay he wrote on the ideal garden, looks at each month in turn to see 'what things of beauty may be then in season'. Apart from roses, stocks (known then as gillieflowers), monkshoods, poppies and hollyhocks, he is able to list no flowers after June and has to be content with a catalogue of fruit alone. It is curious that apart from poppies, annuals do not seem to have occurred to him. Love-in-a-mist, larkspur, nasturtium and the common marigold were all in circulation by the end of the sixteenth century, and Tusser's *Five Hundred Points of Good Husbandry* had recommended that some plants such as larkspur (or lark's heel) 'should be set in Spring and at Harvest time in pots, pailes or tubs or for summer in beds', which suggests that summer bedding was not totally unknown in Elizabethan England.

Flowers could not be relied upon to keep spring eternal, but greenery would never fail. Green was the colour of spring and of life, so evergreens were highly prized. Sir Philip Sidney's Arcadia boasted 'continuall greenes' and no garden was properly furnished without its share of conifers. It is recorded that Sir John Lucas of Colchester had to resort to cutting branches of fir, lashed to the branches of his leafless trees, to prepare his garden for a winter visit from the king's mother-in-law, Marie de Medici, in 1638. He was an exception. Most gardeners in the seventeenth century seem to have planted a generous proportion of evergreens.

By the end of the century Timothy Nourse was writing of an idyllic country house garden 'with Flowers for every month or season of the Year' and 'a Grove of wilderness ... made to represent a perpetual spring'. Of the flower borders at equal distances, he wrote, 'let there be little bushes of evergreens as Dwarf Cypresses, Philyreas, Rosemary, Lavender, Bays, Lawns, Limes, Savine and Rue; for these also are Green in winter and sticky.' This gives us a remarkably clear picture of trim bushes of aromatic shrubs, set regularly in the empty beds in winter and adding substance to the flowers in summer. 'In the grove there are tufts of cypress trees; laurels, Philyreas, Bays Tumarist, ... Pyracantue, Yew, Juniper, Holly, Cork tree and in a wood with all sorts of winter Greens ... Also up and down let there be little banks or hillocks planted with wild thyme, violets, primroses, cowslips, daffadille, lilies of the valley, blew bottles [bluebells – not flies], Daisies, with all kinds of Flowers which grow wild in the Fields and woods; as also among the shades strawberries, and up and down the Green-Walks let there be good store of Camomile, water mint and origany and the like; for these being trod upon yield a pleasant smell; and let the walls be planted with Hedera canadensis and Philyreas and C.'

Italian cypresses were also much more common than they are today. The Italian cypress dominated gardens in the first half of the seventeenth century, but a succession of cold winters in the 1680s made gardeners nervous of relying on these trees again,

Tunnels of limes trained over poles provide shade from the sun at Hatfield House. At Theobalds, the important Elizabethan garden which also belonged to the Cecil family, but now no longer exists, you could walk for two miles in the shade.

55

The Oxford Botanic Garden was founded around 1620. Although the layout has changed a little, plants are still grown in families, like these modern irises. The plant connoisseurs of the seventeenth century grew as many as twenty different sorts of iris in shades of pink and blue. The disadvantage of the modern hybrids is that their leaves die back after flowering. An old variety which has attractive foliage is Iris pallida. Iris florentina, which provides the orris root for pot-pourri, is also dependable, if less flashy than the descendants of today.

especially as clipped specimens. After this disappointment native yew was found to be a much more suitable plant for the art of topiary, which continued to be a popular feature throughout the seventeenth century. There are views of Oxford colleges seen over a period of fifty years which chart the growth of this craze and show how much 'cut greens' increased up to 1700. No garden was complete without its population of closely trimmed specimens.

Much of the credit for introducing the evergreen yew must go to John Evelyn, whose *Sylva or a Discourse of Forest Trees*, published in 1664, was the reference book most widely consulted for almost a century. Its author was a combination of all that was best in Restoration England. A scientist and Fellow of the Royal Society, Evelyn kept bees in a glass hive in his own garden and conducted experiments in a laboratory. He designed a heated greenhouse and wrote books on forestry and gardening. He was also public-spirited; he was commissioner for London streets, for charities, for the Dutch war wounded, for the Mint, for trade and for plantations. Somehow he also found time to travel and to write books about architecture and sculpture and he designed gardens which looked beyond the narrow confines of French formality.

Evelyn added something extra to the enlightened gardens of the other gentlemen scientists and moralists of his time. The natural philosopher's gardens which he made for himself at Sayes Court at Lewisham and for Lord Arundel at Albury in Surrey really belonged more to the eighteenth century than the seventeenth century, for he had tired of:

> those painted and formal projections of our Cockney Gardens and plotts, which appeare like Gardens of past board and March pane, and smell more of paynt then of flowers and verdure: our drift is a noble, princely, and universall Elysium, capable of all the amoenities that can naturally be introduced into Gardens of pleasure, and such as may stand in competition with all the august designes and stories of this nature, either of ancient or moderne times; yet so as to become usefull and significant to the least pretences and faculties. We will endeavour to shew how the aire and genious of Gardens operate upon humane spirits towards virtue and sanctitie, I meane in a remote, preparatory and instrumentall working. How Caves, Grotts, Mounts, and irregular ornaments of Gardens do contribute to contemplative and philosophicall Enthusiasms; how *Elysium, Antrum, Nemus, Paradysus, Hortus, Lucus,* &c., signifie all of them *rem sacram et divinam;* for these expedients do influence the soule and spirits of man, and prepare them for converse with good Angells.

The gardens derived from French inspiration had never been spiritual places; while the smaller gardens and orchards of the gentlemen scientists and plant collectors were perhaps more moral than philosophical. Evelyn's contemplative and philosophical enthusiasms corresponded more to the mood of the Italian gardens which he had visited on his travels. There, reflection and repose were more important than French display or scientific curiosity. Those who made the Grand Tour pilgrimage in the years after Evelyn's death in 1705 would turn his dreams of Elysium into reality.

CHAPTER 3

TEMPLES, IDYLLS & SERPENTINE CURVES

'Glorious Nature supremely fair and sovereignly good'

The Queen's Theatre from the Rotunda, Stowe House, Buckinghamshire *by Jacques Rigaud (1681–1754)*

G ARDENS WERE FOR SO LONG CONSIDERED AN EXTENSION OF
the geometry of buildings that they were slow to take on a unity of their own. In
his work upon *The Gardens of Epirus: or of gardening in the year 1685* William
Temple displayed an early hankering for discarding the ruler and the compass
when he wrote of the charm of asymmetry. He never went to China, but from
descriptions of gardens there and from a familiarity with the 'less obvious beauty
of this kind: that is without order', which he had seen on gowns, screens and porcelain
from India or the Orient, he gave some thought to whether this departure from formality
might also be helpful in garden design. 'But', he concluded, 'I should hardly advise any of
these attempts in the Figure of Gardens among us, they are Adventures of too hard
Achievement for any common Hands; and though there may be more honour if they
succeed well, yet there is more Dishonour if they fail and 'tis twenty to one they will;
whereas in regular figures tis hard to make any great and remarkable faults.'

In a large seventeenth-century drawing of his own garden at Moor Park in Surrey
(named after the Earl of Pembroke's house in Hertfordshire which Temple admired) there
is a wavering path through an irregular patch of land which lies outside his typical
seventeenth-century formal gardens. This is one of the earliest recorded examples of a
serpentine path in an English garden. 'Regular figures' would continue to appear around

*Opposite: William Kent started life as a painter. His
knowledge of perspective and chiaroscuro gave him
a sure hand with different shades of green. At
Rousham in Oxfordshire he used all the tricks of the
painters' and stage designers' trade.*

59

The terrace walk at Farnborough Hall in Warwickshire shows an early stage in the transition from formal garden to natural landscape. The levelled grass walk has temples at either end, but looks out over the countryside. In the mid-eighteenth century all this land would have been grazed and not ploughed.

houses all over the country for years to come, but their geometry was doomed. Sir William Temple's flirtation with asymmetry was only one of many signs that by the end of the century experiments with the wavy line would be found all over England.

Gardens in the French style were still being made by the designers who were in favour at the turn of the century. One of these was Henry Wise, a partner in the Brompton Park Nurseries, who succeeded London as Royal Gardener. Wise was not one to depart from 'regular figures'. He gained his reputation by being more frugal than London and he was a good horticulturalist. One of his first jobs for Queen Anne was to arrange for all the hedges to be dug up because the queen disliked the smell of box.

Another partner at the Brompton Park Nurseries was more interesting. Stephen Switzer had literary inclinations, Sir Thomas Browne and Milton were among his favourite authors, and he wrote thoughtfully about the making of gardens. 'Why should we be at that great expense of levelling of hills or filling up of Dales when they are the Beauty of Nature?' he asked. Design, he thought, should submit to nature and not nature to design. He liked formality near the house, but 'extensive gardening' was what he practised further out. This meant relying on little natural coppices, as well as large woods and cornfields, which he thought were as delightful as the finest garden. He did not want to see all the beauty of a garden at once and he called for the unbounded felicities of a distant prospect.

Such specific criticism of a style that had prevailed for so long was unusual, but there were others who felt equally strongly. Like an orchestra tuning up, they were murmuring phrases from a symphony that was about to be given in concert and heard all over England.

There were many reasons which contributed to this desire for a different tune. The start of a new century meant a fresh start in everything. The French influence on all of fashion, including gardening, which had been so strong throughout the Stuart reigns, seemed to have lost its appeal with a new dynasty on the throne. However, historical perspective allows us a glimpse of Louis XIV telling his architect Mansard at Versailles to lighten the baroque style with a dash of *jeunesse*. It also shows us the beginnings of that rococo style which was to abandon order for asymmetry. Some French influence may well have been acting undercover, despite contemporary claims to Francophobia. Indeed the gardening manual which was found in many country house libraries was still French: *The Theory and Practice of Gardening*, written by D'Argenville, was translated by John James and appeared in 1712. Addison, who was a champion of the sort of gardening which Switzer proposed, had a copy of this work and so did John Aislabie, whose garden at Studley Royal in Yorkshire can still be seen today.

The Theory and Practice of Gardening recommended parterres, groves and palisades to screen views of undesirable woods and mountains and all its design precepts were great

The curve of terrace at Rievaulx in Yorkshire, like the one at Farnborough, was designed to provide a series of views as you walked along it. A particular feature of this changing landscape was the ruined Abbey in the valley below, which can still be seen today.

The tradition of the hero fading into the sunset may not have been familiar to Kent, in spite of his theatrical leanings. However his placing of this statue at Rousham, whether intentional or not, is beautifully stage-managed for a twentieth-century audience.

We know that Kent once spent all night alone in the Temple at Chiswick. He may also have enjoyed the rising of the sun at Rousham.

The watery staircase of the Cascade at Chatsworth was designed by a pupil of Le Nôtre in 1701, but in spite of their grandeur these formal waterworks began to look rather out of place by the middle of the eighteenth century, when many fountains were replaced by waterfalls and canals were turned into lakes. The Cascade House at Chatsworth was designed by Thomas Archer, who had water piped under the floor of the house inside so that surprise fountains could soak the unsuspecting visitor.

Opposite: John Aislabie, the disgraced Chancellor of the Exchequer at the time of the South Sea Bubble, retired to Yorkshire to create his garden at Studley Royal. All his life the purchase of the ruin of Fountains Abbey eluded him, but after his death his son was able to complete the transaction and buy the focal point of the view up the valley.

and noble. It did, however, contain one very modern idea. 'At the termination of walks . . . we frequently make through views, with a large deep ditch at the foot often lined on both sides to sustain the earth . . . which surprises the eye upon coming near it and makes one cry "Ah Ah" from whence it takes its name.' Much later, Horace Walpole in his *History of the Modern Taste in Gardening* (1771–80) was to refer to the 'ha ha' as the simple enchantment that set the garden free from its prim regularity.

The interest of literary men played an important part in the rebellion against geometry. Gardening today is not an intellectual pursuit, nor is it much concerned with taste. In the eighteenth century, taste was an obsession and poetry, painting and gardening ranked in the same league. Pope described Charles Bridgeman, who succeeded Henry Wise as Royal Gardener in 1728, as 'another man of the virtuoso class as well as I, and in my notions of the higher kind of class, since Gardening is more antique and nearer God's own work than poetry.' Bridgeman, had some intellectual pretensions, although he was not himself a writer of note. His only published work was a report on the Bedford Level but among his friends, as well as Pope, he numbered Matthew Prior, Kent and Vanbrugh. As a designer, he belonged more to the new than the old century. He pushed out the frontiers of gardens by using the ha ha, he directed walks to views of open country with cultivated fields and he swept away parterres and replaced them with lakes. 'He had', said Walpole,

'many detached thoughts that strongly indicate the dawn of modern taste.' Bridgeman's greatest work was done at Stowe, where he collaborated with Vanbrugh.

At the same time as Bridgeman and Switzer began to blur the outlines of formality, the theory of garden making began to be questioned. Learned and literary articles were published in various places on the topic of Nature versus Art. Lord Shaftesbury philosophized about 'Glorious Nature, supremely Fair and sovereignly Good' and questioned the peace of mind of a grandee with a great garden in the French style. Addison wrote essays in *The Spectator*, where he fantasized about a happy region inhabited by the goddess of liberty and observed that 'there is generally in Nature something more grand and August than we meet with in the curiosities of Art'. Pope wrote in *The Guardian* of his own garden and ventured that:

> I believe it is no wrong Observation, that Persons of Genius, and those who are most capable of Art, are always most fond of Nature, as such are chiefly sensible, that all Art consists in the Imitation and Study of Nature. On the contrary, People of the common Level of Understanding are principally de-lighted with the Little Niceties and Fantastical Opera-tions of Art, and constantly think that *finest* which is least Natural. A Citizen is no sooner Proprietor of a couple of Yews, but he entertains Thoughts of erecting them into Giants, like those of *Guild-hall*. I know an eminent Cook, who beautified his Country Seat with a Coronation Dinner in Greens, where you see the Champion flourishing on Horseback at one end of the Table, and the Queen in perpetual Youth at the other.

Pope's own garden may not have been adventurous by our standards but it had trees and shrubs around a large lawn, where a formal grove stood. There was no parterre and no topiary. An obelisk to his mother ended the garden, while urns and statues closed other vistas. It was not a garden for show but a place for reflection. It also fulfilled his own three rules of gardening: 'the Contrast, the Management of Surprises and the Concealment of Bounds'.

The thoughtful gardeners who emerged at the beginning of the eighteenth century took as their inspiration the idyllic places described by Horace or Virgil. Milton's passage about Eden, in *Paradise Lost* was also sacred to the early landscapers. Then:

> Flours worthy of Paradise which not like Art
>   In Beds and curious knots, but nature boon
>   Poured forth profuse on Hill and Dale and Plaine
>   Both where the morning Sun first warmly shone
>   The open field, and where the unpierst shade
>   In around the noontide Bours: This was this place
>   A happy rural seat of various view.

Spenser was another source of inspiration. Kent, whom Walpole later crowned 'king of the modern taste', painted some illustrations for the *Faery Queen*, and Bridgeman we know was given a folio copy of the same work by Matthew Prior. William Kent brought another element to the revolution in aesthetics. He was a painter who had lived in Italy where he studied the idealized landscapes of Claude and Poussin. Like Addison, who went

Opposite: The front drive at Chicheley Hall illustrates the pull of the central axis which dominated early garden layout, before circuit walks and serpentine curves became fashionable.

67

Above: The lead statues at Melbourne, like most seventeenth- and eighteenth-century lead figures, were probably painted white to look like stone. Or they may have been coloured 'with an intention to resemble nature', as they were described by one visitor to a sculptor's yard in the mid-eighteenth century, but they would not have been left in their natural state.

Left: All Loudon and Wise gardens had plenty of statues and ironwork. At Melbourne their aim was 'to suit with Versailles' and the plan was in the style of Le Nôtre. Lead statues by Van Nost, like this Mercury, furnished the walks and lawns.

At Stowe some of the trees which were planted in the first quarter of the eighteenth century have had to be replaced. This avenue is modern, but it gives a much better idea of what an avenue looked like in its owner's lifetime than the fully grown overmature trees which date from the original planting.

to Italy to 'compare the natural face of the country with the landskips that the rocks have given us', Kent looked at the Italian *Campagna*. He also looked at gardens with Lord Burlington, who became his patron after meeting him on the Grand Tour. On his return to England Kent took up architecture and interior decoration and with the help of Lord Burlington, he found work in several large country houses. At Lord Burlington's own house, Chiswick Villa, Kent softened the early garden and incorporated some Italianate features. As a painter, he had studied the effects of perspective and chiaroscuro. He applied the techniques of painting to bring light, depth and shade to gardens that lacked variety, even though they relied on colour from flowers. Kent used different shades of green and was a master of that art of 'Contrast' which Pope had declared one of the first rules of garden making. Indeed the 'opening and retiring shades' of Venus' Vale at Rousham in Oxfordshire reminded Walpole of Pope's garden and made him wonder whether the poet's modest garden at Twickenham had not inspired Rousham, 'the most engaging of all Kent's works'.

Like a painter who develops a particular style, Kent managed to put his own stamp on a landscape. Certain things were recognizably Kentian: loose groves of trees on a hill framing a view; or trees scattered at the margin of a stream bore his mark; while water, which for so long had been straightened and formalized, was freed by him and 'taught to

serpentine'. From Italian gardens, which were much more theatrical than French ones and from his own work as a designer for the stage, Kent would have been at ease with Pope's second rule 'the Management of Surprises'. The strange rococo rill or stream in the wood or the *trompe l'oeil* cascades at Rousham were dramatically different from anything else seen in England at that time. The enchantment of a space, the poetry in a garden, which so many writers had tried to promote, was effortlessly, stage-managed by Kent. From the lessons he had learnt from studying paintings and from his own work as an artist he could organize images which would make others respond in the same way as they might when looking at a landscape, or reading about Arcadia.

'English gardens', wrote Goethe, meaning English landscape gardens, 'are not made to a plan, but to a feeling in the head.' Kent specialized in feelings. He once spent all night alone in the temple at Chiswick. Was he perhaps one of the earliest Romantics? Pope's last precept 'the Concealment of Bounds' was also fulfilled by Kent, or rather he did not conceal the bounds, but simply did away with them by bringing the countryside into the garden. In Walpole's words he leapt the fence and saw that 'all nature was a garden'. He dealt in no colours that were not nature's and used no lines that were not wavy, for nature, he knew, abhors a straight line. By adopting some early vertical thinking about concealing the bounds, Kent also managed to satisfy all those who had been singing nature's praises so

Loudon and Wise worked at Melbourne Hall in Derbyshire, which is one of the rare grand gardens of England to have kept its very early eighteenth-century layout.

Kent rearranged Bridgeman's earlier layout at
Rousham so that the visitor looks down on to the
river from this arcaded viewpoint, the Praeneste.

loudly. He was inefficient and impractical. He laid his gardens out without line or level and his knowledge of horticulture was minimal, but Walpole's assessment of him, 'that he struck out a great system from the twilight of imperfect essays' still stands.

The presence of a genius often heightens the performance of others. By 1750 gardening was the topic of the day. A host of like-minded professionals and amateurs had set about building and planting in various corners of England, and several of them had by that time turned their possessions into 'a pretty landskip' (with temples) or a *ferme ornée* (with animals) depending on their inclination and their purse. On the grandest scale, Vanbrugh had helped Lord Carlisle, at Castle Howard, and the Duke of Marlborough, at Blenheim, and Lord Cobham, at Stowe, to monumental splendour. Joshua Reynolds was later to describe him as 'an architect who composed like a painter'. At Stowe, which was to become one of the most talked-about landscapes of the whole century, he provided a glut of temples and a pyramid. At Claremont in Surrey, which was once his own, he made a belvedere, and at Blenheim, one of the grandest bridges in Europe. In 1709 he was pleading with the Duchess of Marlborough to keep the distant and ruined manor house at Blenheim, because it was an ancient building and had historical associations. A glimpse of building in a thicket of trees would make up for the deficiencies in nature on an ungovernable hill, he argued, and it would make one of the most agreeable objects that the

The amphitheatre at Claremont in Surrey was designed by Bridgeman to look over a round pond. This was turned into a lake by Kent, who was frequently called in to blur the edges of Bridgeman's work.

best of landscape painters can invent. Vanbrugh took surprise to the point of drama and in his sense of a national, rather than a classical, past he brought to the English landscape early intimations of all the unknown forms of the Gothic. Landscapes with ruins came later and when they came they were often totally fake, like the Abbey at Painshill in Surrey, or they boasted sham improvements like the decorated mill cottage which Kent used, around 1740, as an eyecatcher beyond the garden at Rousham.

During the years between 1722–42, a curious and difficult man, who had once joined Vanbrugh in trying to save the Holborn Gate in Whitehall, was manoevering to secure the grandest Gothic ruin of all, Fountains Abbey, to complete his garden vista. John Aislabie had been Chancellor of the Exchequer at the time of the South Sea Bubble. He spent a couple of years in the Tower and then retired in disgrace to his estate in Yorkshire, where he set about cultivating his garden. His father-in-law, Edmund Waller, had owned a fine formal garden in the south of England with a temple, by Colen Campbell, where Aislabie must have acquired a taste for landscaping. Studley Royal, which Aislabie laid out himself, became one of the most famous and visited gardens of the eighteenth century. Lord Hardwicke thought 'the natural beauties of Studley were superior to anything of the kind I ever saw', and today the combination of a steep-sided natural valley ending in a view of sublime ruins has lost none of its power to move. In an age when essayists from Burke to

The banker Henry Hoare created a Classical circuit of temples at Stourhead in Wiltshire. Here he created a Virgilian Walk, with temples inspired by the paintings of Claude and Poussin. Later his descendants planted ornamental trees and shrubs around the lake; in spite of this Henry Hoare's idyllic vision still survives intact.

The amphitheatre at Claremont in Surrey represents thousands of eighteenth-century man hours. Today earth moving can be done with machinery in a couple of days.

Addison devoted pages to analysing the qualities of the sublime, the sight of Fountains must have intensified all those emotions and feelings which were the subject of so much intellectual speculation. The purchase of the Abbey eluded John Aislabie all his life and was only secured after his death and added to the property by his son, so it was always out of reach of the early visitor to Studley Royal. The enchantment which distance lends can never have been so well illustrated.

The sublime, with its overtones of terror and pity, hardly seems apparent at Stourhead in Wiltshire today, where people go to see autumn colour or rhododendrons or to have a family picnic by the lake. This romantic circuit of temples was laid out by another amateur 'gardenist', the banker Henry Hoare, over a period of about thirty years. It was started some twenty years after Aislabie had begun his work at Studley Royal. Today the buildings are agreeable incidents on an afternoon's walk, but Henry Hoare meant them to be far more than that. They are the totems of one man's culture, the icons of an age. Addison suggested that there were three writers in the learned languages who excelled at opening a man's thoughts and enlarging his imagination. Of Homer, Virgil and Ovid he wrote 'the first strikes the imagination wonderfully with what is Great, the second with what is Beautiful and the last with what is Strange.'

Although this essay was written thirty years before Henry Hoare began his garden,

the ideas contained in it were generally current among civilized men throughout the first half of the century. 'Reading the *Iliad*', he observed, 'is like travelling through a Country uninhabited, where the Fancy is entertained with a thousand Savage Prospects of vast Desarts, wide uncultivated Marshes, huge Forests, mis-shapen Rocks and Precipices. On the contrary, the *Aeneid* is like a well ordered Garden, where it is impossible to find out any Part unadorned, or to cast our Eyes upon a single Spot, that does not produce some beautiful Plant or Flower. But when we are in the *Metamorphosis*, we are walking on enchanted Ground, and see nothing but Scenes of Magick lying round us.'

For the garden maker, Virgil or Ovid clearly have more to recommend them than Homer. Henry Hoare demonstrated his classical learning by creating a series of tableaux which were chosen to suggest the sixth book of Virgil's *Aeneid*. At one level it was like a classical treasure hunt, with the odd clue in the form of a Latin tag, to encourage the onlooker to recognize scenes from the poem, but more than an intimate knowledge of Aeneas' journey to the underworld was demanded of the visitor. On reaching the Pantheon at Stourhead where, in a building like a Greek temple beside an English lake, Hercules was enshrined, it was not enough to recall the qualities of the demi-god and his claims to a place in the Pantheon as the role model for Aeneas: there were perhaps more private challenges to the knowledge and imagination.

It was to Studley Royal in Yorkshire that John Aislabie, the disgraced Chancellor at the time of the South Sea Bubble, retired to lick his wounds and cultivate his garden. The formal water and lead statues look back to the French style, but the temple in the trees suggests Italy and the paintings of Claude. The gardens were an innovation in their day and marked the transition to a wilder, more natural style of gardening.

Overleaf: The Octagon Tower at Studley Royal is seen against a backdrop of Scots pines, which were a favourite eighteenth-century tree. Wordsworth preferred it 'to all other trees except the oak, taking into consideration its beauty in winter, and by moonlight, and in the evening.'

The Palladian bridge at Stowe, like the one at Wilton, was designed to be seen from a distance. These ornamental bridges were places for reflection, in both senses of the word.

Previous page: Temples like this one at Rievaulx were meant to be seen against a backdrop of evergreens. Holly, yew, holm oak, Portugal laurel, arbutus and the now rarely used phillyrea were all used to set off garden buildings.

Today Hercules is best remembered for his superhuman strength. We connect him with strangling snakes and cleaning stables, but at the time of the classical revival in the eighteenth century the attributes which he suggested were virtue and piety. Lord Burlington owned a painting of the *Choice of Hercules* by Mattei which had been commissioned by Lord Shaftesbury to illustrate an essay on 'the Notion of the Historical Draught or Tablature of the Judgement of Hercules'. The story, taken from Xenophon's *Memorabilia* (II, 6,22), comes from a dialogue between Socrates and Aristeppus about the education of the young and is not now well known. In it, the young Hercules is offered a choice between two feminine personifications of vice and virtue. Virtue, which he chooses, tells him about the toil and effort of a virtuous life, suggesting among more spiritual precepts that 'if you want of land to yield you fruits in abundance, you must cultivate that land; if you are resolved to get wealth from flocks, you must care for those flocks.'

The primary aim of a landscape garden in the early eighteenth century was to set up a chain of associations and reflections on poetry and art. The connections between Lord Burlington and Hoare were close; not only did the creator of Chiswick bank at Hoare's, but Henry Hoare's daughter Susannah married the heir to Lord Burlington's Irish titles in 1753, the year in which Burlington died and also the year of the first recorded payment for the building of the Pantheon. A collection of associations which included Socrates,

Xenophon, Burlington, Mattei, Shaftesbury, Virtue and the apt quotations about fruits and flocks were all proper subjects for reflection at the temple of Hercules.

In addition to all this classical impedimenta, the sight of the Pantheon was also meant to be the starting point for another series of associations (connected not with literature but with painting). The Pantheon, or temple of Hercules, which was designed by Henry Flitcroft for Henry Hoare was based on two paintings by Claude. A copy of Claude's *View of Delphi with a Procession*, which was known to have been owned by Hoare, had a similar temple, as did the more famous coast view of *Delos with Aeneas*, which Hoare may well have seen in Paris where it was up for sale in 1748. This painting formed one of a series – inspired by the artist's admiration for Virgil. They were his interpretation of the scenes which were so familiar to the educated classes.

Claudian images of Arcadia, and idealized versions of temples in a landscape, are fleetingly seen in other early eighteenth-century landscape gardens, but Stourhead is perhaps the only one where Claude is imitated so clearly. Stourhead is the landscape of the painting, of the landscape – with the artist's gloss on *The Aeneid* thrown in for good measure. Such double entendres, echoing ancient authors, would not have been lost on Stourhead's early visitors. The book of the film of the book is an amusing conceit for us, but it would have intrigued our ancestors more, steeped as they were in classical learning and

At Stourhead in Wiltshire the Pantheon conjured up a whole series of associations. This temple was sacred to Hercules, who is today best remembered for his strength, but at the time of the Classical revival the attributes which he suggested were virtue and piety. The primary aim of a landscape garden was to set up a chain of reflections on literature and art.

dedicated to Plato's philosophy which traced all beauty back to a single source of perfect form. Pope compared his own grotto to the cave in Plato's *Republic*, where flickering images of reality appeared on the darkened walls. The mirror images of ideal beauty, as interpreted by Claude, would have made good conversational fodder at Stourhead. Other painters were also acknowledged in Henry Hoare's garden. In a letter to Lady Bruce, he described the part of the garden where 'the view of the Bridge, Village and Church altogether will be a charming Gaspard picture at the end of that Water', and the statue in the river god's care was, as the late Kenneth Woodbridge, the garden historian, points out, modelled on a figure of Tiber, in a Salvator Rosa painting of the *Dream of Aeneas*.

These examples only illustrate a sample of the poetic and painterly references at Stourhead where natural phenomena would also have been laid out to prompt memories and provoke association. Walpole quoted lines from *Paradise Lost* when he looked at the river at Stourhead; others unrecorded may have resorted to Virgil as they stood by the lake or in the wood. In gardens today the game of cultural one-upmanship is played with Latin plant names; in George II's day the challenges were more varied. References to literature, painting and England's historic past were all common. The Bristol Cross at Stourhead and Gothic temples in gardens all over England were the reminders of our national heritage which Vanbrugh had urged on the Duchess of Marlborough. Ruins and heritages nudged

Claudian images at Stourhead would have been recognized and enjoyed by Henry Hoare's friends. In the house hung a copy of Claude's 'View of Delphi with a Procession' showing a similar temple to this one designed by Henry Flitcroft.

Opposite: The temples at West Wycombe were staging posts along the circuit walk, providing a view of the next destination. From the Temple of the Winds, the Cascade beckoned and beyond that were Kitty's Lodge and Daphne's Temple. Most modern gardens lack temples, but the principle of leading the eye on to the next treat can still be observed.

the onlooker to thoughts of *sic transit gloria mundi* (thus passes all earthly pride and glory) and if they looked like a Piranesi or a Clérisseau, so much the better. In nature's monochrome gardens the colour came not from flowers but from the rich variety of references. (Even the plants had associations. White poplars were sacred to Hercules who is often depicted crowned with a wreath of poplar leaves).

Stourhead is one of the best examples of the type of garden which presented a carefully arranged sequence of eighteenth-century cultural markers, but it was not unusual in its day. The Elysian Fields at Stowe were packed with layers of meaning. Allusions to politicians of the time, a representation of Addison's allegorical dream of liberty in a garden and an illustration of Lord Cobham's family motto *templa quam dilecta* (how lovely are thy temples) were all there to be read, as well as the more conventional references to classical and painterly terms. At Chiswick many of the 'quotations' were architectural to illustrate Burlington's particular interest.

In other gardens acknowledgements to even more private preoccupations might be made. A figure of Flora might have the face of the owner's wife or a mistress and if the authority of the architect Batty Langley's *New Principles of Gardening* (1728) allowed for a statue of Nillo in the paddock or the wilderness ('a famous Glutton who used himself to carry a calf every morning until it became a large Bull, at which Time he slew it with his Fist and eat him all in one day'), who knows what scope there was for representing enemies or ludicrously greedy friends?

Fashionable sentiments called for an expensive outlay on masonry, and gardeners of more modest means than the banker Hoare had to display their high-mindedness in economical ways. William Shenstone was a poet with an income of only £300 a year. He made a garden in Warwickshire which was famous for its poetic associations. Using plaques with mottoes, as well as seats and urns at strategic places, he manipulated the minds of visitors to his garden with much the same effects as did the owners of larger estates. His account of a conversation following a tour of his property by Mr Lyttleton and James Thomson, the poet, allows the twentieth-century reader to eavesdrop on the making of this type of garden. 'I told him my then intention of building a model of Virgil's Tomb; which with the obelisk and a number of mottoes selected from Virgil together with the pensive idea belonging to the place might vindicate ... the appellation I had given it. Thomson assented to my notion of taste in gardening ... he denominated my Virgil's Grove then Le vallon occlus – Sombre says Mr L. – No, not Sombre, occlus – this must evidently be the idea of Petrarch's Valclusa. He recommended a walk *up* that valley from Virgil's Grove.' Poor Shenstone; his finances were considerably worse than Hamilton's and creating Virgil's Grove ruined him. Samuel Johnson summed up his sad end in his *Lives of the Poets* when he wrote, 'He spent his estate in adorning it and his death was probably hastened by his anxieties.'

By 1753 the adornment of estates became a national craze, but in the wrong hands the poetry could turn to doggerel and the painting to a 'chef d'oeuvre of modern impertinence'. 'Grotesque little villas which grow up every summer within a certain distance of London, are fatal proofs of the degeneracy of our national taste', commented *The World*, a satirical journal of the day, which went on to ridicule the nouveaux riches for their slavish imitations of the fashionable style, who in two acres of ground crammed all the incidents which had come to be expected in a garden of taste. 'A yellow serpentine river stagnating through a beautiful valley, which extends nearly twenty yards in length ... A grove perplexed with errors and crooked walks ..., an old hermitage built with roots of trees, which the saviour is pleased to call St Austin's Cave ... and ... a pompous clumsy and gilded building, said to be a Temple and consecrated to Venus' guaranteed a place for

the owner 'on the most conspicuous stage which Folly can possibly mount to display herself to the World.' If two generations of intellectualizing about aesthetics had made temples too popular it was perhaps time to shed pretension and return to grass roots.

The view of Chicheley across the canal is dominated by a Cedar of Lebanon. These trees were introduced towards the end of the seventeenth century, but the true cedar of Lebanon is now hard to obtain. The blue Atlas cedar is not an acceptable substitute.

CHAPTER 4

CLUMPS, LAKES &
WAGGONLOADS OF ACACIAS

'High polish and flowing lines'

The garden at Nuneham Park *by Paul Sandby*

I
N THE TWENTIETH CENTURY WE SAY TOLERANTLY 'THERE IS NO accounting for taste' because we no longer share a common fund of aesthetic principles. We would find it hard to understand a code of taste laid down by an autocratic élite as it was in the eighteenth century. Royalty and aristocrats are not now credited with setting the examples for a style of living which it is social death to ignore. Design today is as varied as the structure of our society. In the reign of the Georges, the patronage of a leisured class was scattered all over England; they demanded quality in everything and only their aspirations were acceptable. It was a time when ordinary builders took their patterns and proportions from the classical orders which were admired by the élite and there was a unity of design in all household objects which is incomprehensible today. The landowning and educated classes set standards of absolute taste in all art forms until the end of the eighteenth century, and gardening was no exception. Popular gardening hardly changed at all for centuries. The unfashionable were condemned to growing a few vegetables and outmoded flowers as they had quietly done for hundreds of years.

In the middle of the eighteenth century three-quarters of the population lived in the country and were dependent on the land for their living. Agricultural techniques were improving, and in the century from 1696 to 1795 two million acres of woodland and wild

Opposite: The Gothic Temple at Painshill Park in Surrey was derelict, but has now been sensitively rescued from decay. It forms one of the set pieces in Charles Hamilton's landscape garden, which has undergone a remarkable restoration.

The picturesque ravine at Belsay in Northumberland was a subject for romantic contemplation. Brooding alone in massive places was popularized first by Salvator Rosa and later by Lord Byron.

land were turned over to farming. Nature was gradually changing, from an incomprehensible and occasionally frightening force, to a civilized ally that brought prosperity to the landowner and a livelihood to the great majority of the English. The course of the relationship between man and nature can be traced very clearly in gardens. The angular gardens of the past which stamped civilized geometric shapes over the wild countryside were laid out to prove that man could subdue nature – with some effort. Once the human upper hand had claimed a wider area, the dogmatic man-made lines started to disappear. The new mood was at ease with the countryside. This was partly due to the reforms in agriculture, but new ideas on nature and liberty were also changing attitudes. Nature, which Shaftesbury had written about so enthusiastically at the turn of the century, was like a stranger at first who had arrived with the recommendation of those old friends, literature and painting. They smoothed the passage of introduction and through their agency the countryside was interpreted and heard. By the middle of the century nature had become more like an old friend herself, who no longer needed the company of others to guarantee her respectability.

The relationship was still being defined by intellectuals, but in a different way. Fields, woods, streams and hills were now thought beautiful for themselves and, more, they were also good for the soul. Rousseau's novel *La Nouvelle Héloise*, published in England

in 1760, may not have been in every landowner's library, but the ideas which it contained were in the air. This work focused on an idyllic country life (without temples) where the characters owed their virtue to the fact that they were far from the corruption of civilization. The emphasis in Rousseau's writings was on primitive innocence and intense personal experience, not shared cultural knowledge. These themes and man's spiritual relationship with nature were at the heart of the Romantic Movement, which endorsed the simple life and a universal language. Before the century was out the queen of France would dress up as a milkmaid, Gainsborough would take to painting peasant families and Wordsworth and his friends would depart for the hills. The contrived and objective verse of the Augustans was slow to abandon itself to romantic subjectivity, but the new sort of gardens were to prove exciting territory for poets, by engaging their private moods in ways which they had never done before. The landscape was no longer to suggest to the observer a series of framed images of a distant country, peopled by gods and goddesses; it was to be a place where a man could walk and think, preferably alone. In some ways gardens turned to romanticism before poetry or politics, but if they appeared to be rejecting Claude's, in favour of clouds, this was only superficial. Claude's paintings continued to exercise their spell on British culture and on attitudes to landscape long after his temples were banished from our gardens.

A winding path under a light canopy of green at Studley Royal in Yorkshire allows views into the valley where the moon pool glitters.

*The Cascade at West Wycombe has been restored
and the original lead statues replaced with
fibreglass ones. A restoration can often be nearer in
spirit to an original work. It is worth remembering
that buildings and statues were starkly new in their
day. The patina of age lends a romance to all old
buildings which was never part of their original
aura.*

The lake at Painshill lies at the centre of the landscape which occupied Charles Hamilton's thoughts throughout most of his life. The garden was a great influence on Henry Hoare at Stourhead, but it finally took its toll of Hamilton's finances and ruined him.

The large landowners were still the people whom everyone wanted to copy. Communing with Nature was not perhaps their first aim; it was not as important to them as 'improving' their land. Henry Hoare overheard William Beckford of Fonthill in Wiltshire say that land he then trod on (in 1764) was improved from thirteen pence halfpenny to twenty shillings per acre. Current overt preoccupations were with drainage and crop rotation; better farming methods gave landowners larger incomes and no doubt they enjoyed contemplating the source of their rising prosperity from their modern well-lit houses. Whether consciously or not, they increasingly chose a man to lay out their gardens and parks who could display this source of wealth but who also brought them closer to nature by making fewer claims upon the intellect.

Lancelot Brown was not bookish and he had no artistic pretensions, but his tact, intelligence and natural 'eye' made him a compelling adviser. He came of yeoman stock from Northumberland and taught himself the principles of architecture, as well as how to draw and survey. His talents soon attracted the attention of Lord Cobham at Stowe, who appointed him his head gardener and clerk of works. By the end of Brown's life he had turned his hand to tasks as varied as rebuilding a church, as he did at Croome in Worcestershire, or enlarging a house, as he did at Corsham Court. Humphry Repton, the great landscape gardener at the turn of the next century, later acknowledged Brown's building work and thought he was, Repton added, 'inferior to none in what related to the comfort, convenience, taste and propriety of design in the several mansions and other buildings which he planned.'

Brown felt that it was important that the landscape designer should site a building, as well as having some say in its design. His buildings were useful, suitable and elegant: dairies, pineapple houses and orangeries soon began to take the place of inscriptions, temples and statues, but at what Brown excelled was making the best of the landscape. When he said that he saw 'capabilities' in an estate, he was only reiterating what Pope had earlier described as 'consulting the Genius of the Place'. However, Brown could make a garden which transformed the particular and regional qualities of the landscape into an idealised conception of nature without the help of any poetic or artistic props. This was very different in its end result from the early landscape gardens, but it still fulfilled Pope's three precepts. 'The Contrast' was provided by what Brown referred to 'as infinite delicacy of planting, so much Beauty depending on the size of the trees and the colour of their leaves to produce the effect of light and shade'. By colour, he meant generally green. Purple or variegated trees were rarely part of his palette. In the 'Management of Surprises' Brown was probably less theatrical than Kent. The scale of his landscapes was certainly surprising and there was often enough water to provoke amazement, but the dispositions of grass, trees, water and sky were gently punctuated by elegant buildings which suggested pauses rather than exclamation marks. 'The Concealment of Bounds' was where Brown really succeeded as more and more land was 'emparked' and brought into the view. Grass came right up to the windows of the house. Terraces, parterres, mounts and palisades were finally abolished and sheep or deer replaced flowers everywhere.

Pure landscape did not prove to be cheaper to arrange than the gardens of masonry and plumbing which had cost earlier landowners so much money. The new Back to Nature style was very expensive. Brown thought nothing of rebuilding a village if it was in the view, as he did at Milton Abbas in Dorset and at Sledmere in Yorkshire. At Milton Abbas some of the villagers were disinclined to move to make way for a lake and had to be flooded into submission by their landlord, Lord Milton. Brown's influence must have been considerable. Other landowners agreed to the levelling of hills to reveal a view of a river, as at Chatsworth; or the building of a new kitchen garden far from the house where its wall would not intrude on the view, as at Basildon in Berkshire, none of which can have been cheap. Almost all of his clients were persuaded that water was an essential feature in the landscape. If no river existed, there was usually a lake in the middle distance whose end could not be perceived. Eighty acres of water was possible on Brown's scale of operations. The levelling, digging, draining and planting involved in creating one of these landscapes represented thousands of man hours.

Legions of trees were planted to frame views and make shadows, not in avenues, but in belts and clumps and dots. Single mature trees from an avenue, or from a line of uprooted hedge, were often left to give age to a landscape and occasionally these were moved. Brown had designed a contraption for levering large trees into their new positions which made this comparatively easy. The belts of trees consisted mainly of mature trees like oak, beech, chestnut and elm, underplanted with birch, hazel, larch or Scots pine to shelter the more important and permanent trees. Some poplar and whitebeam were also used, as well as plenty of ilexes and yews, especially near the edges, to make shadows. The outlines of the woodland were blurred by the odd single tree standing out from the group. Christopher Hussey, who wrote about landscape, suggested that the young plantations must have looked tight and

A modest temple at Painswick in Gloucestershire sits quietly among the laurels, providing a resting place for contemplation on the tour of the garden. In the eighteenth century the laurel chosen was often the smaller leaved cherry laurel, rather than this glossy version.

Statues under trees suggest contemplation. At Mottisfont in Hampshire, where people flock to see the roses every summer, there are still corners of the garden which evoke a less sensual response.

stiff in their cattle-proof fences and the appearance of a Brownian park was probably much tidier than modern examples which have been softened by the patina of decay. There was no dead wood in a Brown-inspired landscape; grass was shorn; riverbanks were clean cut and bare of undergrowth. Golf course and public park standards of maintenance prevailed. Because people only see a legacy of large trees in eighteenth-century parks, they often assume that these are all that was intended, without realizing that the more detailed planting has disappeared. In the wildernesses surrounding the large trees, which were then in their infancy, all sorts of shrubs grew along the winding paths. Brown added climbers like honeysuckle for scent as well as lilacs, laburnums and roses (sweetbriar, *Rosa mundi*, 'Maiden's Blush' and 'York and Lancaster' were all specified at Petworth) and sumach, maple, the native butcher's broom, spiraea and hawthorn were also included for variety.

At Kedleston in Derbyshire, which was not designed by Brown, but by William Emes who worked in his style, bills survive for 1760 which list 1000 lilac syringa *Philadelphus* and several hundred laburnum, as well as 350 honeysuckle, roses and unspecified flowers for planting the Long Walk. At Hatchlands in Surrey, Admiral Boscawen's wife Fanny ordered 700 similar plants which were raised in boxes by the gardener to complete her 'walk' in 1756. Our woodland gardens are versions of these eighteenth-century shrubberies, which, apart from the kitchen garden where flowers were grown for the house, contained the only flowers in the gardens of Brown and his followers. The modern woodland garden however is much more relaxed and natural in its layout than most eighteenth-century wildernesses; then trees and shrubs were planted at regular distances, one of a kind, not grouped, and they were graded in height.

James Meader, who ended up working for Catherine the Great in Russia, had been the Duke of Northumberland's gardener; he wrote a *Planter's Guide or Pleasure Gardener's Companion* in 1779. 'Capability' Brown worked for the Duke over a period of about thirteen years from 1760–73 both at Syon and Alnwick, so Meader must have worked from Brown's directions. His instructions throw an interesting light on plant grouping towards the end of the century. The book is no more than an alphabetical list of hardy trees and shrubs for ornamenting parks and pleasure grounds, but the short introduction is informative, for James Meader's reason for compiling such a book is that recent planting 'which at much labour and expense have of late and former years been executed ... will be found on examination to be very injudiciously arranged ... owing to an improper inter mixture of the plants.' Deciduous trees were often commonly mixed with evergreens, but, he suggested, would be better separated into clumps which is what gentlemen of taste practised in their plantations. The Duke's late gardener liked to see the largest and tallest trees at the back and close together. Deciduous trees could then be moved, 'particularly forest trees most of whom will bear removal at a very considerable size' and could be used to embellish parks either singly or in clumps. He suggested that shrubs and smaller trees should be planted at their final distances and that the spaces between them should be occupied by 'perennial, biennial and annual flower plants: which, while the shrubs are growing, will not only fill up the vacancies, but be very ornamental to the new plantation.'

Meader also enclosed a plan for 'The Disposition of deciduous trees and shrubs for a Plantation' which has 171 plants, ranged in seven rows in graded height. Each plant is different and not clumped as he suggests. Lilac, daphne, jasmine, roses, spiraea, rhododendron, syringa (philadelphus), hydrangea, rubus, honeysuckle, lavatera and tamarisk were some of the more familiar plants included. There is a similar plan for an evergreen plantation, with six rows of planting, which includes a few flowering shrubs like honeysuckle, which seems to have been a universal favourite, as well as brooms, cistus, medicago and rhododendron (rosebay). These arrangements are not at all natural but they

were typical of their time. Throughout the eighteenth century stepped or graded plantations were seen everywhere. Batty Langley recommended this style of planting, as did Philip Miller, curator of the Chelsea Physic Garden, whose *Gardener's Dictionary* was the leading reference book on cultivation and design from 1731 onwards.

The 'high polish and flowing lines' of the fashionable landscapes laid out by Brown and his followers, like William Emes and Richard Woods, would also have been copied in smaller gardens by those who did not employ designers. In Suffolk, in the wet summer of 1784, three young Frenchmen on a prolonged visit to England made a new garden walk for their host. With the help of two servants they dug a path half a mile long and four foot wide. It took them fifteen mornings to do the work in three hours before breakfast, but at the end of the operation they felt that they had learned, both in theory and in practice, the art of the English garden. Some of the minor gentry and clergy made miniature landscapes for themselves with curving belts of shrubberies at the edges of their properties where a circuit walk might be taken.

In these smaller gardens, which appear in paintings of the period (like the naval captain's house in Kent painted by Serres in 1777 or the archbishop Samuel Foote's house in London attributed to de Bruyn in 1767), there is much close-mown grass around the house and it all looks very tidy and sparse. For similar gardens, where shrubberies were

The remodelling of the garden in 1770 at West Wycombe Park in Buckinghamshire, by a disciple of Capability Brown's, loosened up the earlier formal layout. During this period Revett designed the Music Temple for the island on the lake, so that it would be seen from the house. It was a place to take an elaborate picnic and lead the sort of simple life which Rousseau recommended.

The magnolias in cultivation in the eighteenth century were mainly the evergreen sort, although Magnolia acuminata which was introduced by John Bartram in 1736 is deciduous, but not very free-flowering. Gardeners such as James Hamilton, who grew all the newest introductions from North America, would have loved the modern forms like this soulangiana hybrid at Oare House in Wiltshire.

being planted, nursery lists indicate that around 200 flowering and evergreen shrubs were available cheaply. Dr John Harvey gives us a clear idea of what was being grown in ordinary gardens from the contemporary bills and the commercial lists of provincial nurserymen towards the end of the eighteenth century. Telfords of York, for instance, listed forty roses in 1775. These and flowering almond, guelder rose, jasmine, laburnum (in bush form), Spanish broom, hibiscus, bay, lauristinus, philadelphus, hollies, bladder sennas, pyracantha, daphne and several sorts of honeysuckle would all have been common in small, as well as large, gardens. In Fanny Burney's diary for 22 March 1794 we learn that M d'Arblay's garden, although still in its early stages, possesses all the common favourites. M d'Arblay's 'greatest passion is for transplanting. Everything we possess he moves from one end of the garden to another, to produce better effects. Roses take the place of jessamines, jessamines of honeysuckles and honeysuckles of lilacs, till they have all danced round as far as the space allows; but whether the effect may not be a general mortality, summer only can determine.'

A Yorkshire parson's plant orders over three years from 1763–66 are a good sample of what must have been grown in rectory gardens all over England. The Rev Thomas Metcalfe ordered plenty of vegetable seeds and some vegetable plants (cabbage, lettuce and cauliflower) and in each of the years recorded he listed fruit. The peaches and apricots and

nectarines which he ordered must have been doubtful, even on walls, in Yorkshire. The shrubs ordered by Mr Metcalfe (in the autumn of 1764) were 'two Syringas, one cytissus, one Persica jasmine [*Syringa persica*], two Mezereons [*Daphne mezereum*], one Hypericum Foutox [spiraea], one Gelderose, one purple and one white lilac, and two double Flowering thorns'. Two years later the nursery that sent his fruit order gave him a free bundle of flowering shrubs which included elder, bladder sennas, Spanish brooms, currants, dogwoods, viburnums and 'striped' sycamores. 'Striped', or what we now call variegated, plants were popular for plantations. There were gold and silver striped chestnuts, striped-leaved elms, striped elder (this was in James Meader's model plantation), striped nightshade, and gold and silver periwinkles on offer in trade lists. Purple leaves were still relatively unknown. The copper beech was a recent introduction and at five shillings each, compared with ten shillings for 1000 one-year-old green beech seedlings; in 1777 their price must have been discouraging. Hardy exotics were even more expensive. At fifteen shillings for a *Magnolia virginiana*, or seven for a *Magnolia grandiflora*, these plants must have been out of reach of most people, yet the number of new plants available for gardeners was steadily increasing and by the turn of the century would become within reach of the majority.

By 1771, when Philip Miller retired from the Chelsea Physic Garden over 5000

Popular roses in the eighteenth century were 'Rosa Mundi', the 'Portland Rose', 'Variegata di Bologna' and 'York and Lancaster'. Sweetbriar was also planted in quantities in shrubberies (but the single blood red Rosa moyesii *in the foreground was not discovered until the end of the nineteenth century). Here it is seen at Docwra's Manor in Cambridgeshire.*

This path through a shrubbery with roses, foxgloves and hardy geraniums at Flintham in Nottingham-shire is not unlike the effect intended by eighteenth-century planters. The plants, except the foxgloves, are modern varieties but the spirit is the same.

different species were recorded. Many of these had come from North America, where for thirty years the Quaker botanist John Bartram had been collecting on behalf of rich patrons. He founded one of the first botanic gardens in America and sent back enormous quantities of plants, including in the 1730s, magnolias, kalmias and rhododendrons which were increasingly, if expensively, planted in gardens like Painshill or Whitton which belonged to the Duke of Argyll. On Bartram's death many plants from his famous collection went to Kew. Sir Joseph Banks, as Director of the Royal Gardens at Kew and President of the Royal Society, was also instrumental in encouraging plant collectors to range further in their search for botanical treasure. With such a disparate array of plants to choose from, it was no wonder the Duke of Northumberland's ex-gardener tried to rationalize their display.

There were, of course, plenty of old-fashioned smaller gardens which had not been 'improved' by the middle of the century. The owners of these were not consciously against Brown; their passive provincial attitudes probably resisted change for reasons of economy, as much as conservatism. Gilbert White, the curate who kept a diary of events in his garden from 1751 to 1768, interpreted the modern taste in a way which had something of the earlier static tableaux style, while still owing a little to the axial geometry of the last century. He cut a vista through several hedges placing his gates to lead to a silhouette of

Hercules on a painted board. He had a voguish ha ha and a hermitage, but he could not resist old-fashioned flowers which he kept unfashionably close to the house. There may have been many like Gilbert White who borrowed a little from the modern taste for 'improving', while keeping elements of the 'nice old place' that Mrs Jennings admired in *Sense and Sensibility*, which had 'great garden walls that are covered with the best fruit trees in the country: and such a mulberry tree in one corner! Then there is a dovecote, some delightful stewponds and a very pretty canal; and everything, in short, that one could wish for ...' There were others, though, who were actively critical of the austerity of Brown's landscapes which had influenced so many into abolishing all decoration and variety in their gardens. For these, mown grass and infant plantations were definitely not enough.

William Chambers, the architect who fell under the spell of China, had no liking for Brown. In their first professional feud he had to concede a commission when Lord Milton, who found Chambers difficult to deal with, allowed Brown to design his village at Milton Abbas in 1763. The rivalry between the two men increased when Chambers was working for Princess Augusta at Kew while Brown was surveyor to His Majesty's Gardens at Hampton Court in 1764. Five years later, matters were not improved between the two men when, in a straight contest to design a new house for Lord Clive at Claremont, Brown's plans were preferred to those of Chambers. Chambers though younger and less successful

Less colourful weeds than these foxgloves at Belsay in Northumberland were encouraged to seed themselves in the foreground of the picturesque landscape. Nettles and burdocks were particular favourites for adding interest and perspective to the view.

than Brown could not accept that his rival was qualified to be an architect. He also felt that he had some pretentions to landscape gardening himself because of his devotion to China. There was a school of thought dating back to Sir William Temple's early conjectures about Oriental style, that the Chinese influence had made a major contribution to the change in English taste. Sir William Chambers was an authority on Chinese gardens and their diversity, and how the Chinese 'like the European painters composed different sorts of scenes; the pleasing, the horrid and the enchanted.' He launched an attack on Brown with a *Dissertation on Oriental Gardening* published in 1772. Brown's gardens, he complained, were exhausting and uncomfortable, like 'large green fields feathered over with a few straggling trees and verged with a confined border of little shrubs and flowers', where the stranger 'finds nothing to delight or amuse him, nothing to keep up his attention or excite his curiosity, little to flatter the senses and less to touch the passions or gratify the understanding.'

Although his theories were based on an accepted tradition, the taste for Chinoiserie as practised by Chambers with Royal Approval at Kew was on the whole judged to be too whimsical for that elegant age: it was less taken up in gardens than it was in other spheres. Walpole greeted the *Dissertation* with scorn. (There are sentences in the essay which are more entertaining than practical – 'European artists must not always hope to rival Oriental

The Ruined Abbey at Painshill, like many other ruins, was a sham. Piranesi and Clérisseau's paintings often set the mood for scenes of decay, which were re-created out of doors.

Opposite: Capability Brown's high polish and flowing lines did not suit everyone. Devotees of the picturesque preferred crags and untended places to the smooth shorn lawns and elegant restraint of Brown's landscapes. At Belsay this sort of effect comes easily. It is harder to achieve in the Home Counties.

At Bowood in Wiltshire the cascade which was built by Capability Brown was altered by Charles Hamilton, the creator of Painshill, and made to look more like a painting by Poussin.

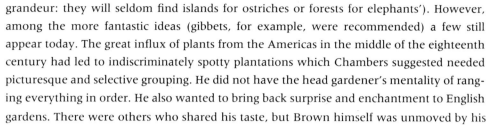

grandeur: they will seldom find islands for ostriches or forests for elephants'). However, among the more fantastic ideas (gibbets, for example, were recommended) a few still appear today. The great influx of plants from the Americas in the middle of the eighteenth century had led to indiscriminately spotty plantations which Chambers suggested needed picturesque and selective grouping. He did not have the head gardener's mentality of ranging everything in order. He also wanted to bring back surprise and enchantment to English gardens. There were others who shared his taste, but Brown himself was unmoved by his critics. He probably felt as he did when admonished by an officious Clerk of the Board of Works for neglecting the gardens at Hampton Court. 'You will be so good as to inform the Gentlemen of the Board of Works', Brown wrote, 'that Pique I pity, that ideal power I laugh at, that the Insolence of office I despise and that real power I will ever disarm by doing my duty.'

Not much evidence survives of flower gardens which resisted the landscape movement, but several paintings of gardens in Berkshire and Oxfordshire indicate that such gardens did exist and that they were different from those of the last century. Contemporary writings about Philip Southcote, who married the Duchess of Cleveland, and his civilized band of friends, among whom he numbered Lord Petre and Joseph Spence the poet, suggest that there must have been many more. Some of the rococo paintings of Thomas Robins show circular or kidney-shaped flowerbeds on the lawns, or among the trees of the gardens he painted. One of these belonged to Richard Bateman, who lived at Windsor, and was described as 'a kingdom of flowers, waggonloads of acacias, honeysuckles and syringas'; this was designed by Thomas Wright, who was an astronomer and garden adviser. His plan for a garden at Badminton in 1750 (which was never adopted) was the antithesis of Brown's work. It was axial, decorative, enclosed and flowery. A series of watercolours by Paul Sandby show an elaborate flower garden at Nuneham Courtenay in Oxfordshire laid out for Lord Harcourt by William Mason, Poetry Professor at Oxford, with long-range advice from Rousseau. This arrangement of island beds was modelled on Julie's garden in Rousseau's famous novel, and may have been influenced by Sir William Chambers's flower beds at Kew. The planting was done in lines which echoed the shape of the beds, with the tallest plants at the centre and the smallest on the edge. A description of similar flower beds in a garden not far from Nuneham Courtenay had a hollyhock or a sunflower in the middle, grading down to alternate clumps of violets and mignonettes in the front row, which sounds to us rather like parks maintenance work, but was probably thought sensitive in its day. Herbaceous plants only started to appear in nurserymen's catalogues after 1782, so the plants for Mason's garden, which was made around 1760, are likely to have been grown from seed.

Growing flowers was one way of reacting to Brown's austerity. Another reaction to the 'high polish and flowing lines' of his landscapes came after he died in 1783, from devotees of the 'picturesque'. Uvedale Price and Richard Payne Knight were close friends and neighbouring landowners who lived in Herefordshire. They demanded more of their gardens than smooth elegance and they attacked Brown and his followers hard – in print. As a child Uvedale Price had been taken for walks by Gainsborough who was a family friend. They brought home 'roots, stones and mosses from which he formed, and then studied foregrounds in miniature'. The adult Price reverted to Claude and Salvator Rosa for 'picturesque' inspiration, but perhaps the experience of watching Gainsborough make miniature landscapes with 'bushes of moss and lichens' and 'distant woods of brocoli' may have subconsciously influenced him in his condemnation of Brown.

Gainsborough is not generally credited with having influenced garden making in England, but it is interesting to note that he was commissioned in 1767 by Lord Shelburne to paint three pictures for Bowood in Wiltshire 'intended to lay the foundation of British landscapes'. Capability Brown worked at Bowood, and his clients were well pleased with him from all accounts. He finished there in 1768 and in 1785 the cascade which he had built was altered to look more like a Poussin, by Charles Hamilton of Painshill. Exposure to the romanticized and picturesque landscapes of Gainsborough may have made the original stones for the head of the water look too plain. Similarly, it is tempting to see Gainsborough's influence at work at Belvoir, where Brown was called in to remodel the grounds in 1779 just after the young Duke of Rutland inherited the title. The plans were drawn 'all very descriptive, fair and neat', but rejected. As Charles Manners, the Duke had bought the painting *The Woodcutter's Return* by Gainsborough. Brown's landscapes may well have started to look uncompromising to more than the vociferous minority in the last quarter of the century. But whereas Gainsborough's approach might have been responsible for subtle and unacknowledged changes in taste, the Rev William Gilpin had a much more didactic approach which caused a fashionable stir.

Brought up in the rugged countryside of the Borders, Gilpin preached the grandeur of remote scenery in Wales and the Lake District and popularized looking at landscapes with the critical eye of a painter. Claude glasses, which were darkened mirrors for inspecting the perfect view, were held up to mountains and lakes by dilettanti everywhere; so absorbed was Thomas Gray the poet that he fell down while using his glass in the Lake District. Gilpin's *Picturesque Tours* written in 1772 were required reading for the fashionable; in *Northanger Abbey* the unsophisticated Catherine Morland is quite lost when she hears the Tilneys on the subject of the picturesque, 'viewing the country with the eyes of persons accustomed to drawing and deciding on its capability of being formed into pictures with all the eagerness of real taste'. The familiarity with the natural world acquired in the domestic and polished landscapes of Brown and his followers had been outgrown. Those in search of a larger canvas were now brave enough to venture further from home into a wild and sublime unknown. The ideologists and artists were finally about to depart, leaving the English garden to become, for a time, a less contentious place.

CHAPTER 5

TERRACES, SHRUBBERIES, ROCKERIES & ROSES

'I like a fine prospect, but not on picturesque principles'

St James' Square, Bristol: the potting house *by Pole (c. 1806)*

WHEN THE AESTHETES WALKED OUT OF THE GARDEN TO abandon themselves to the call of the wild, who was left to fill the vacuum created by the pure curves and bland spaces of Capability Brown? At the beginning of the Napoleonic Wars there were two factions contending for the English garden. The devotees of the picturesque, the seekers after melancholy and ruins, still wanted to make Brown's tame green fields look like a painting by Salvator Rosa. This was all very well in the borders of Wales or Scotland, but it was not very suitable for the flatter land of the Home Counties, where the old order was changing fast. The merchants and stockjobbers who were covering the green fields round London with their new villas had no traditions of country life and no room to display their culture out of doors in the way that the old landowners had done. Picturesque qualities were as difficult to accommodate in a two-acre landscape as the earlier fashion for temples and grottoes had been. Decay and neglect could only be absorbed in very large places where hovels or stagheaded trees might represent picturesque incidents in the middle distance, but their contrived untidiness was depressing at close quarters. Weeds were unacceptable in the foreground: the obligatory burdock or nettle, which was such a help to the artist's perspective, was not an adornment to the lawn. 'I like a fine prospect but not on picturesque principles. I do not like crooked twisted blasted trees. I do not like ruined tat-

Opposite: Straight paths, roses and trellis had been banished from the landscape to the privacy of the walled kitchen garden. Repton reintroduced all these into gardens around the house in the early years of the nineteenth century. Here at Castle Howard in Yorkshire the same features furnish a walled garden in twentieth century style.

The garden at Sezincote in Gloucestershire was
made to surround a nabob's mansion. Thomas
Daniell, the painter of Oriental scenery, supervised
the planting and the layout. Below an elephant
bridge lies a dark pool, surrounding a snake
fountain. Graham Stuart Thomas advised on the
planting at Sezincote during the 1950s and '60s
and the lush waterside plants add an extra layer of
history to this Mogul fantasy. Primula florindae,
the giant cowslip, was found by Kingdon Ward in
Tibet in 1925.

tered cottages. I am not fond of nettles or thistles or heath blossoms. I have more pleasure in a snug farmhouse than a watch tower and a troop of happy tidy villagers pleases me better than all the banditti in the world,' says Jane Austen's hero in *Sense and Sensibility*.

Feelings too had outgrown the landscape. Gentle melancholy had been easy enough to suggest; an ivyed urn in a dark corner was a discreet reminder of the grave, but images of the more subjective agonies of 'being' needed space and stranger backgrounds. Salvator Rosa's lone figure brooding among boulders was better translated by the verses of Byron than by introducing chaos into a corner of the garden. Claude's pastoral scenes in antique landscapes had lost their allure and Faerieland had replaced antiquity as the desired landscape. *The Enchanted Castle*, the most popular Claude at the turn of the nineteenth century, was widely available in an engraved version, which must have debased its visual potency, but its thrill was recharged by poetry. Remoteness and Faerieland were subjects for Keats (or the Gothic lady novelist Mrs Radcliffe); they did not fall within the scope of the private landscape. It was as though the magic had vanished from gardens and parks. All the feelings which they had been able to summon in the eighteenth century were now better evoked by literature. 'Ordinary landscapes remind us of what we see, in the country, Claude's of what we read in the greatest poets and of *their* perception of the country,' wrote Samuel Palmer in the first quarter of the century. This statement could not have been made a hundred years earlier. Constable's criticism of parks for their lack of spiritual quality was similarly modern; remarks like these signalled the end of the tradition of the garden as a place for contemplation or culture. Changing patterns of thought also shifted the emphasis in man's relationship with nature; the primrose by the river's brim might reveal its divine purpose to Wordsworth, but to the new breed of gardener it was a source of a different sort of worship – the worship of plants.

The plant cultists were the other strong contenders for a place in the garden. Throughout the eighteenth century there had been growers of 'curious' plants who had financed botanical expeditions and raised rare trees from dust-dry seeds in their own gardens; they were the heirs of the gentlemen scientists in Restoration times. All through the years of the landscape movement they had been quietly cultivating their gardens and exchanging notes and cuttings with one another. There were men like the unfortunate Charles Hamilton at Painshill, who spent all his money on the making of his garden which finally bankrupted him. He introduced rhododendrons and azaleas into this country as well as many North American exotics. He took trouble to grow things properly and was interested in the science of cultivation, even corresponding with a French abbé about how best to grow vines in Surrey. In Yorkshire there were squires like William Constable who studied botany and competed with his neighbours to grow the most pineapples, while another northerner, Dr John Fothergill, took his medical practice to London, where he made enough money to create a botanical garden for himself at East Ham. He kept an unparalleled collection of exotics in a huge glasshouse.

Of all these plantsmens' gardens little now remains; but the botanical drawings of Ehret and those who were influenced by him record enormous numbers of plants which must have been grown in gardens all over England. Amateur botanists, like the Duchess of Beaufort at the beginning of the century and the Duchess of Portland later on, encouraged the collecting, dissecting and growing of rare and curious flowers. The Duchess of Portland's friend Mrs Delany, whom Dr Johnson described as 'the highest bred woman in the world and the woman of fashion of all ages', spent her declining years making portraits of around 1000 flowers in meticulous botanical 'cutouts'. Many of the plants which Mrs Delany recorded were found at Bulstrode, where she often stayed

with the Duchess of Portland, but she also took her material from lesser gardens when she visited other friends.

These people were the forerunners of a new sort of gardening where collections of plants would assume more importance than either sensations or picturesque scenes. Horticultural novelty was set to take over from the absolute standards of taste which had gone unquestioned for so long. This fragmenting of aesthetics was also reflected in the breaking up of the old social order. Just as the purity of absolute taste was being diluted and changed, so the old landowning aristocracy were losing their supremacy. Adult education, getting on in business, technical knowledge and domestic comfort were some of the agents in the melting pot which caused a change in the chemistry of society and all of these were also to affect the way in which people treated their homes and gardens in the years to come.

Almost at the turn of the century, a man appeared who fused all these different elements together, bringing a judicious direction to the art of landscape design. For a brief patch at the beginning of the nineteenth century Humphry Repton held on to the best of eighteenth-century standards, with a leavening of nineteenth-century preoccupations. His balance of art and nature has rarely been equalled. Garden making over the years could be likened to a seesaw with nature at one end and artifice at the other. The seesaw was firmly

The Camellia House at Chiswick is one of the first ornamental greenhouses in England. Its dome is now much reduced but it originally had stained glass panels and was designed by Samuel Ware, who was responsible for the Burlington Arcade. In 1825 Loudon described the conservatory as 'the most gloomy we have seen', but ten years earlier, when it was built, it was an innovation. Camellias are no longer considered hot-house plants, as they were shortly after their introduction in the middle of the eighteenth century.

Wistaria first flowered in England in 1819 when it cost six guineas to buy this expensive introduction from China. The form grown then would have been blue. This long white-flowered variety seen at Somerleyton Hall in Suffolk is a later introduction.

Opposite: Wistaria can be shy to flower, sometimes taking as long as ten years before it settles down. Side shoots need shortening hard at the end of the summer and again in late winter to encourage flower buds to form. Here it grows well on an arch at Shute House in Dorset.

held down by artifice during the time of the architectural gardens, until the eighteenth-century landscapers transferred all the weight to nature's end. Then Repton jumped on to the middle of the seesaw as nature was about to fly up in the air again, to straddle the two extremes.

Humphry Repton was born in Norfolk in 1752. He was brought up to be a cloth merchant but when his father died he gave up trade, at which he was never much good, and retired to the country where he concentrated on civilized pleasures. Here he read widely and met and corresponded with scientists and botanists and he learned how to manage his small estate. He was as pleasant and accomplished as any eigtheenth-century gentleman. He wrote light verse and was, according to a contemporary, an ingenious, easy, witty and graceful letter writer. He danced well, he played the flute and he sketched and painted delightfully. His nineteenth-century virtues were that he was exceptionally practical (except in the management of his own financial affairs) and when his money dwindled and he was forced to move his large family into a cottage he did not repine. A cottage he claimed, was 'a dwelling where happiness may reside unsupported by wealth'.

He made the best of his life and in true entrepreneurial style, spotting a gap in the market after the death of Capability Brown, he woke up one morning at the age of thirty-five and announced that he was going to be a landscape gardener. (He was the first

Repton loved Sheringham in Norfolk best of all his commissions. Abbot Upcher, whose house it was, wrote in his diary 'Repton decided on the spot and the approach, for which I shall never cease to thank him, and those who come after me, conscious of the blessing of being screened from the snowy north, will learn perhaps to thank him also – and will they hallow the memory of Abbot Upcher whose pride it is to have been the founder of his Family at Sheringham?'

119

The garden at Sezincote was probably laid out by Repton, with directions from Thomas Daniell, after he returned from India with a portfolio of Oriental views. Sacred bulls, serpents, shrines and Mogul arches were all incorporated in this Gloucestershire garden.

person to apply the phrase to himself.) He at once sent out circulars for commissions from all his acquaintances and was soon rewarded with plenty of work. His agreeable and cheerful manners quickly advanced his career, for he knew how to be polite to everyone; he was tactful about the deficiencies of some of the places where he was consulted, while making the most of others. He encouraged owners to think for themselves, often basing his suggestions on their ideas and flattering their taste. His gardens were made for people and for their use and enjoyment. 'Convenience ought to take the lead in a constant residence, since picturesque effect is too dearly bought at the price of comfort', he wrote in his proposals for *Honing in East Anglia* in 1792.

In 1794 he made a list of the 'Sources of Pleasure in Landscape Gardening' which demonstrates how carefully he selected all the best qualities from preceding styles. On his list were many old favourites and a few new ideas. The catalogue began with 'Congruity' and was followed by 'Utility, Order, Symmetry, Picturesque Effect, Intricacy, Simplicity, Variety, Novelty, Contrast, Association, Grandeur, Appropriation, Animation and Seasons'. 'Congruity' and 'Utility' put people first, while 'Order' and 'Symmetry' bowed to the gardens which existed before the tidal wave of landscape swept discipline away. 'Picturesque Effect', 'Intricacy' and 'Variety' gave a nod to fashionable taste, but 'Simplicity', 'Association' and 'Grandeur' looked back to the gardens of Brown and before.

'Appropriation' and 'Animation' suggested all that belonged to an estate and the life that went on there, and this anticipated the cosy domestic tradition which would later dominate nineteenth-century home life. With his final bow to the seasons, Repton introduced the idea of change into gardens. No longer was a garden to be seen as a frozen set piece, but as a process of evolution.

Here there was a suggestion of gardening in addition to garden making, which was new. Repton did not have the single-minded vision of his predecessors, but he was dealing with a much more complicated brief than any they had tackled. His civilized compromises made for comfortable arrangements out of doors which certainly satisfied the clients. A typical customer, Pole Carew, wanted Repton to improve all Cornwall and kept him up to date with marriages and deaths which might lead to opportunities for improving estates. Within six years of his decision to take up the practice of landscape gardening Repton was the acknowledged expert and had written a book of sketches and hints on the subject. Jane Austen wrote about him and Thomas Love Peacock satirized him; for the layout of a garden was still a topic of general interest which deserved a passing mention in the contemporary novel.

Repton brought people back into the garden. He gave his clients terraces in front of their houses so that they no longer stepped out of the French windows into a park where

Separate gardens devoted to the collections of flora from one area were often laid out by Repton. There were many places which were devoted to North American or Chinese flowers, but Indian gardens like Sezincote were unusual. It is a disturbing and beguiling place, whose strange shapes, ferns and Orientalia make it very different from most English gardens.

animals grazed. Jane Austen-like heroines, who owned no gumboots and were inconveniently dressed for mud, must have been delighted with the emphasis on gravel walks laid down for the 'essentialy useful' purpose of providing a place to exercise in spring and autumn 'where the heavy dews on the lawn render grass walks almost inaccessible'. Repton thought about the comfort of his clients indoors. He liked to avoid a western aspect because of the discomfort caused by the glare of the setting sun 'given the present late hour of dining'. Outside he provided shade, holding that 'a summer garden without shade is a solecism.' Late in his life when he turned to designing London squares he thought about providing grassy edges to gravel walks 'where children might play, reflecting that in the future this [Russell] square may serve to record that the art of Landscape Gardening in the beginning of the nineteenth century was not directed by whim or caprice, but founded on a due consideration of utility as well as beauty.' Accordingly, he never failed to point out that gardens were for use and enjoyment. In one illustration he even showed the convenience of the raised strawberry bed for the disabled gardener. He took trouble with the siting of kitchen gardens; a good southerly aspect near the stables, where manure was well placed for collection, was generally the best position.

As he grew older he came to recognize the ornamental value of a walled garden and arranged for walks to visit the kitchen garden where the fruit, or a few early flowers in a sheltered border, might be admired. He recommended arches of apples and pears to grow over the paths which would screen the less decorative vegetables from sight and give some shade in summer, like the old covered walks of earlier formal gardens. The ultimate convenience for the client was the manner in which Repton produced his plans. His 'Red Books' were prepared so that they might show the scene before and after 'improvement'. An ingenious flap could be raised to show a smooth curve of water where a shallow, uneven expanse had been. Clumps of trees were thickened, or trellis and flowers added. The text of the written report which accompanied the watercolours was flattering to the client and made a decorative proof of the owner's taste when left lying around on a table for others to admire.

Repton's antiquarian approach to architecture reflected a return to earlier traditions. But as buildings settled into comfortable vernacular styles, the plants out of doors became more exotic than ever. Soon separate gardens were needed to display all these specialized collections of plants. American gardens, Chinese gardens, rose gardens, areas for evergreens, or aquatics, a thornery and an old English garden all began to appear in Repton's designs. There were fifteen specialist gardens at Ashridge. Other gardeners were less selective. Unable to resist the fashion for variety, they crammed one of each plant into their smaller plots. By 1813 the number of plants available since 1789 had doubled. The art of garden making was becoming the science of cultivation and for the rapidly emerging middle class this was a much easier option than Repton's elegant compromise of the picturesque with the horticultural.

After Repton's death in 1818 the Brownian Park was finally killed off as an artistic aim and novelty and whimsical variety emerged everywhere. Even at Chiswick, that bastion of taste in the early eighteenth century, 'the ugly fashion' prevailed. A German visitor, Prince Pückler Muskau, recorded a visit to the garden in 1826 where he saw pleasure grounds planted 'with thinly spaced, almost militarily arranged trees giving the lawns the appearance of tree nurseries. In the shrubberies they prune the bushes all over so that they cannot touch the neighbouring shrubs, carefully clear the earth around them every day and arrange the borders of the lawn in stiff lines so that you see more black earth than green, and the unfettered beauties of Nature's forms are altogether suppressed.'

This rigidly cultivated look obviously needed plenty of maintenance, but labour was still cheap and there was no need to be a duke to be able to pay a gardener. The average suburban homeowner with a couple of acres, a greenhouse, and possibly a conservatory tacked on to the house, would have had a full-time gardener with a garden boy as well. In

the first quarter of the nineteenth century all gardeners, however, required more skills than the scything and trimming which had been all that were needed to maintain a landscape park. Capability Brown's foremen were not required to know much about potting and propagation. Keeping exotic plants alive demands technical knowledge: the professional gardener was an essential ingredient in a garden which relied for its effect on displaying a wide range of plant material. Head gardeners became formidable authorities. At Wilton, Mr Chalice the head gardener used to walk about eight miles round the garden every day in a top hat and tails. In a novel by Emily Eden written in 1830, the heroine walks out into 'a first rate gardener's garden, every plant forming part of a group and not to be picked or touched on any account; all of them forced into bloom at the wrong time of year and each bearing a name that was difficult to pronounce, and impossible to remember. Helen was standing apparently absorbed in admiration of a *Lancifolium speciosum* which she had been assured by her gardener was "a better variety" of the *Lancifolium punctatum* . . .' Poor Helen.

The professional gardener was given plenty of encouragement to develop his knowledge and skill. At the beginning of the century Sir Joseph Banks, the naturalist who sailed round the world with Cook, and a member of the philanthropic Wedgwoods had founded the Horticultural Society; this now offered reduced membership for working

Geraniums were in favour throughout the nineteenth century. Here some older varieties are seen at Northbourne Court in Kent interspersed with silver leaves, which were not as popular in the last century as they are today.

The great Double White rose was widely grown throughout the nineteenth century. It is a strong growing shrub with large creamy scented flowers in June.

The rose garden at Castle Howard in Yorkshire has grass paths between billowing bushes of old roses. The Victorians loved rose gardens and were happy to grow them away from other flowers, an idea first thought of by Repton.

gardeners. In 1822 the first edition of John Claudius Loudon's *Encyclopedia of Gardening* appeared which was designed 'to disseminate new and important information on all topics connected with horticulture and to raise the intellect and character of those engaged in this art'. Loudon was a Scot and a liberal who wrote sixty million words on gardening in the course of his life. He coined the word 'gardenesque', recognizing the need for an expression which would sum up the new attitudes to intensive cultivation. 'By the gardenesque style is to be understood the production of that kind of scenery which is best calculated to display the individual beauty of trees, plants and shrubs in a state of nature; the smoothness and greenness of lawns; and the smooth surfaces, curved directions, dryness and firmness of gravel walks; in short it is calculated for displaying the art of the gardener.'

For 'art', about which Victorian gardeners talked and wrote frequently, modern readers might substitute 'artifice'. Art in the sense that it was used in the preceding century, and perhaps increasingly at the time of writing, was not what the Victorian garden was about. Loudon became the authority of his age. In later life he admired Repton but most of what he wrote was directed at those who had fewer acres than a typical Repton client; *The Suburban Gardener and Villa Companion*, published in 1838, was aimed at the rising middle class. Loudon was high priest of order and efficiency. He graded houses into a social hierarchy from first rate to fourth rate and he commended tidiness wherever he saw it. His tours of English gardens with his wife Jane, who was equally high-minded, provoked comments in the pages of *The Gardener's Magazine* on the example set by others. After ticking off the aristocracy for having gardens scarcely ever seen 'in a state of worse keeping', Loudon wrote in 1833 that the only highly kept gardens which they saw were those of small proprietors, professional men, merchants or bankers.

Mrs Lawrence's villa at Drayton Green comes in for particular praise:

> This place, of limited extent, and possessing no material advantage, except that of a dry soil on a subsoil of gravel, has been rendered a perfect *bijou* of floricultural beauty by the exertions and taste of Mrs Lawrence. All the most rare and beautiful hardy flowers and peat earth shrubs are here assembled, and beautifully disposed in groups, in the natural or picturesque manner, on the smoothest lawn; interspersed with a few trees, and decorated with fountains, statuary, vases, rockwork, and basketwork. There is a green-house full of choice articles; and there is not a plant that is not grown in the very highest degree of perfection, or a scene that is not in the highest order and keeping. Among the plants that struck us as profusely covered with bloom, and beautifully grown, were the single and double *Clematis florida*, the yellow Chinese and yellow Noisette roses, the *Calandrinia grandiflora*, *Petunia phoenicia* and *nyctaginiflora*, all the new *fuchsias*, showy *nicotianas*, *Lupinus mutabilis*, and others.

Descriptions of Mrs Lawrence's garden make it sound much too busy for modern taste, but it was admired in its day and Queen Victoria and Prince Albert paid it a visit. Loudon generally took rather a Calvinist line on attempting too much in a small space, but other even more elaborate gardens which he saw may have made this one seem simple by comparison. Rustic work, that debased conclusion of the picturesque movement, abounded at the Villa Lawrence, and this too Loudon occasionally censured as

Opposite: Repton popularized garden history and this brought about a revival of interest in terraces and topiary. It was a long time, if ever, before the yew in the early nineteenth-century historical gardens reached the scale of Powis Castle.

The Reptonian Pheasantry at Flintham no longer houses birds, but is surrounded by roses and shaded by trees. Compare this with any view of an eighteenth-century temple, when no flowers colour the space around the building. The romantic and sentimental mood of the early nineteenth century made flowers much more acceptable in the landscape.

inappropriately rude or common. From John Buonarotti Papworth, who was an architect as well as a garden designer, we get an idea of how prevalent rustic work was in the time of the Regency. 'Rustic seats, bowers, root houses and other such small buildings now decorate our gardens, when something more in character with the scene ... might be used.'

Jane Loudon shared her husband's mission to instruct and to improve horticulture. Her particular interest was the role of the lady out of doors and she popularized gardening for women 'who might find their health and spirits wonderfully improved by the exercise and by the reviving smell of fresh earth'. *The Ladies Flower Garden* was issued in a monthly series from 1839–48 and this and later the magazine *The Ladies Companion* included topical tips for lady gardeners.

Tips for gardeners of both sexes continued to pour from the pens of the experts. As the century progressed the best head gardeners and nurserymen took to writing up what they had learned from their own practical experience. Joseph Paxton, the Duke of Devonshire's gardener at Chatsworth, had his own botanical magazine and was one of the founders of *The Gardener's Chronicle* in 1841. Paxton's achievements remain a beacon to the self-made man. In addition to his knowledge of plants, he mastered waterworks, forestry and architecture and could turn his hand to design projects as varied as a village, a park, or

a cemetery, as well as to his masterwork, the Crystal Palace. It was hardly surprising that he ended up a knight and a millionaire.

There was plenty for the new experts to cover because the early part of the nineteenth century saw enormous changes in the techniques of horticulture. Diseases of plants were better understood and skills in hybridizing and transplanting were improving all the time, while better greenhouses meant that more plants could be grown in artificial conditions and made to flower out of season. The repeal of the glass tax in 1845 brought glasshouses and conservatories within reach of many new gardeners. All these tricks with plants needed to be displayed in a new way which would draw attention to the triumph of growing them. In 1828 the social commentator William Cobbett had drawn the distinction between 'beds where the whole bed consists of one sort of flower' and 'borders, where an infinite variety of them are mingled together, but arranged so they may blend with one another in colour as well as stature. Beds are very little the fashion now, excepting among the florists who cultivate their choice flowers in this manner; but the fashion has for years been in favour of borders, wherein flowers of the greatest brilliancy are planted so disposed as to form a regular series higher and higher as they approach the back part, or the middle of the border; and so selected as to insure a succession of blossom from the earliest months of the spring until the coming of the frost.' This arrangement of banked plants was a refined

Iron arches on stone pillars support the roses at Newby Hall in Yorkshire. Nineteenth-century rose gardens would have used ironwork for their supports, or occasionally ropes in festoons garlanded by climbers.

A chance seedling from the rose called Maiden's Blush which was often found in cottage gardens, was named Konigen von Danemark after it appeared in 1816. This vivid pink quartered rose is still grown today.

The Victorians, who liked strong colours, would have loved the modern 'Cerise Bouquet' rose, seen here flowering at Flintham Hall in Nottinghamshire, but their palette was restricted to dark reds, pinks, whites and mauves.

Grass paths and lawns in general became much easier to keep after Mr Budding patented the lawn mower in 1830. Before this, scythes were used to cut the lawn and the close and tidy finish recommended by Loudon was almost impossible. This grass path at Newby Hall between hedges of roses takes minutes to mow.

version of the eighteenth-century shrubbery layout recorded by James Meader. It was not found to be the best method for showing off the seasonal blast of colour now being engineered by the horticulturalists. Beds, rather than borders, began to be filled with plants grown under glass in the 1830s. Before this, the occasional pot of tender and temporary flowers had been sunk in the ground to cheer up the shrubbery border. (Chambers had been in favour of this method.) The new-found confidence in transplanting meant that it was now possible to replant a whole bed with plants like pelargoniums, verbenas and petunias. Spring bedding, which relied on bulbs for its effect, was developed in the 1840s.

The beds in the villa gardens which contained these new plants were generally scattered about in the shape of commas, kidneys, circles, stars and moons, or indeed any other shape that appealed to the owners, as though someone had emptied the contents of a kaleidoscope on to the lawn. Larger gardens – especially those designed by William Nesfield, who favoured 'olde worlde' parterres – were more formally arranged. Elaborate patterns of beds like those in seventeenth-century gardens were once again spread out below the main windows of the house. But now dazzling colour added an extra dimension to the complicated layout. At Cliveden, the head gardener specialized in spring bedding; clipped privet and spruce edged the beds, which were filled with rhododendrons and azaleas, as well as a mixture of the brightest spring bulbs and pansies. The plants were arranged in groups of one sort. 'In modern flower gardens, the old practice of having a variety of plants in one large bed and arranging them according to their height and colour, has been entirely superseded, and the system of grouping plants of one sort in small beds substituted for it,' wrote Joseph Paxton in 1838, ten years after Cobbett had recorded borders as the fashion of the day. Colour rather than form was an important feature everywhere in the Victorian age. The demand for brighter colours followed the discovery of artificial pigments for paints and dyes used on walls, fabrics and ceramics inside the house. The management of colour was a popular topic around the middle of the century when head gardeners argued about the merits of complementary colours or contrast and harmony in bedding out.

The rose garden was one of the specialist gardens which appeared almost everywhere. It was more restrained than the 'gay parterre'. 'In the formation of the Rosarium,' wrote a leading nurseryman in 1848, 'it appears to us that the simpler the forms of the beds the better.' Round beds were popular and grass walks were generally preferred to gravel here. Many of the roses were grown as standards and some were trained up posts and along chains to make a scalloped backing for the beds. In 1848 106 Hybrid Perpetual roses and 145 trees were listed by the nurseryman William Paul, as well as large numbers of Damask, Provence, Gallica and Moss roses. Two decades later the number of Hybrid Perpetuals offered by the same nurseryman was 538, almost five times as many. Today the favourite rose of the Victorians is available in less than a hundred varieties. These vigorous shrubs often had their shoots pegged down at the tips so that they made mounds of branches covered in heavy-petalled flowers. Sometimes bushes grown in this way would be surrounded by hoops in iron or wire to suggest the popular shape of a basket. (In the flower garden, 'pincushion' beds gave a similar domed effect). A handle of ivy added the finishing touch.

The rockery was the other specialist area that was common to many gardens. Alpines which had formerly been grown in pots could now have a home of their own, 'frequently', wrote Mrs Loudon, 'arranged according to female taste ... so arranged as to afford a striking object in the landscape; and at the same time, so as to form a number of little nests or crevices for the reception of alpine plants'. Rockeries in their early stages were a debased form of grotto, designed to show off a variety of geological materials. Lava, shells, fossils and flints and collected rocks were all used. Large gardens like Chatsworth used huge boulders. 'The spirit of some Druid seems to animate Mr Paxton in these bulky removals,' wrote the sixth Duke in 1842. The machinery which Paxton devised could move a block of stone weighing fifty tons. Smaller gardens could not run to such a 'picturesque assemblage of natural rocks'. Often they made do with clinker, or vitrified bricks, and even occasionally broken china. In the 1840s rockeries made of artificial stone composed from broken bricks and cement began to be built by James Pulham, whose father had invented Pulhamite stone. 'Rustic work and rock work,' wrote Shirley Hibberd, 'are, I consider in the very worst taste anywhere in front of a neat villa .... I could almost wish that ferns and rockeries had never become fashionable.'

The wild musk roses with their cluster of heavily scented flowers were often found in gardens in the last half of the nineteenth century. This modern variety was a chance seedling at The Old Rectory, Burghfield, and has been named Betty Hussey. It is a particularly good form.

CHAPTER 6

CARPETS OF COLOUR, FOLIAGE & FERNS

'That great plant family which the curiosity of man has discovered and cultivated'

View, Alton Towers *by E. Adveno Brodie (1857–8)*

T HE VICTORIANS, PARADOXICALLY, LIKED SENTIMENT AND SCIENCE. They were also keen on morals, family life and self-improvement. Many of these preoccupations were represented in the mid-Victorian garden, where plants, and more particularly flowers, now absorbed everyone's attention. Publicly, flowers were being used as expensive temporary building materials to create carpets of colour in increasingly complicated patterns. Massed and disposable, they had lost their individuality as plants in a flower bed. The reaction to a display of scarlet geraniums then, as now, cannot have provoked anything more than amazement and a shower of congratulations for the head gardener. His command over unpredictable nature in marshalling the colours was undisputed in the 1850s. The owner of the garden probably gained extra kudos for encouraging a particularly lavish performance, but I dare say nobody wasted many words on the troops of plants which created the effect.

Privately, the attitude to flowers was very different. Indoors, obsessional botanists were examining plants as never before. Botanizing was thought a suitable science for a lady and the Swedish botanist Linnaeus' system of identifying plants continued to be used in drawing rooms long after serious botanists had found better means of classification. Collecting flowers involved long walks and fresh air which were good for the complexion.

Opposite: The Victorian age spanned a huge range of taste. Some of their favourite features are expressed in this picture, which shows the brilliant and exotic colour of rhododendrons above naturalized bulbs at Caerhays.

135

'Few people really care about flowers,' wrote Ruskin. 'Many indeed are fond of finding a new shape of blossom, caring for it as a child cares for a kaleidoscope.' Hybrid rhododendrons and azaleas in ever more brilliant colours found their way into the English garden in increasing numbers after the introduction of the Wardian case, in spite of Ruskin's censorious remarks.

It also provided work for idle hands after the return home; for when the walk was over the flowers could be painted or pressed. Evidence of the industry of countless country ladies lies in attics and drawers today, but not all of them reached such a high standard of watercolour painting as the five Clifford daughters and their two maiden aunts: their *Frampton Flora* records the flowers they found near their Gloucestershire home in the years between 1828 and 1851. Others with less talent shared the same passion for botanizing; for to display interest in this subject was judged a mark of gentility.

Neither the response to the flowers in the 'perfectly dazzling' parterres nor the knowledge gained from detailed inspection in the drawing room can explain the sentimentality which flowers aroused in the Victorians. The plants in their gardens were highly bred and developments in hybridizing brought new varieties every year, which was as remarkable a technical achievement as the head gardener's timing with the bedding out, but it was hardly one to inspire emotion. According to Ruskin, 'Few people really care about flowers. Many indeed are fond of finding a new shape of blossom, caring for it as a child cares for a kaleidoscope ... Many are scientifically interested in them, though even these in their nomenclature, rather than the flowers.' But the strain of sentimentality in descriptions of flowers in the mid-Victorian age belies this remark. 'Laughing rosebuds', 'peeping honeysuckle', 'coy violets' and 'blushing peonies'; flowers were given the most

embarrassing qualities in the literature of the period. 'Queen rose of the rosebud garden of girls', wrote Tennyson. 'The wood anemone may put us in mind of some quiet, shy modest girl who makes all sunny and happy round her,' suggested Charlotte M. Yonge. Forget me nots, which Loudon had referred to as 'this well known sentimental flower' in 1829, were particular favourites. The Gothic legend of the knight who drowned in his attempt to pick this flower for his love might not be so appealing today as it was to the Victorians, who found the combination of death and duty irresistible. The language of flowers was another cult which endowed flowers with more attributes than stalks and stamens. This elaborate method of communication provided a secret code for lovers. A rose was much more than a rose, it could say 'meet me by moonlight' (Rose la France), 'you capricious beauty' (Rose Musk), 'I am worthy of you' (Rose white), to which the reply might be a bunch of rue (disdain), snake's foot (horror) or, more encouragingly, 'I feel the first emotions of love' (Lilac purple).

The precision techniques of bedding out did not suggest flowery compliments or sentimentality, but the overall layout of the garden was increasingly nostalgic. Period gardens which looked back to the formal layouts of the seventeenth century were popular after articles about garden history began to appear in the gardening magazines around the middle of the century. The architect Sir Charles Barry made a trim version of an

Italianate gardens of the nineteenth century used statues and evergreens to look like cypresses, but rarely with roses. The result of using similar ingredients in a modern idiom produces a twentieth-century version of Victoriana at Flintham.

Shrublands in Suffolk was meant to look like an Italian garden. Its wide views and descending terraces were laid out by Barry. The basic ingredients of an Italian garden were a balustraded terrace, plenty of gravel and vertical accents from topiary or cypresses. Often there were fountains.

Opposite: The bedding at Lyme Park in Manchester is not quite as lavish as it would have been in the late nineteenth century, when Lord Newton laid out his 'Dutch' garden. In those days five changes of plants per year were not unusual. Now the colourful display is beautifully maintained, but is only replanted twice a year.

Elizabethan parterre in Lancashire, and Nesfield executed several plans from John James's translation of D'Argenville's *Theory and Practice of Gardening* which had been so often consulted before the landscape movement. Coloured gravels were once again employed to fill scrollls; topiary, mazes and bowling greens were back but Capability Brown was still out of fashion. There was perhaps some confusion about exactly which period to revive. Formal gardens were variously described as Olde English, Elizabethan, Jacobean, French, Dutch and Italian. It finally seemed easier to call them all Italian, for had not Repton suggested that Italian gardens were the mainspring of our own, before the other styles from the Continent became fashionable? This also suited those who favoured Italianate architecture rather than Jacobean. Some gardens were more Italian than others. For Trentham in Staffordshire, Barry with all the enthusiasm of the newly returned traveller, proposed an island to look like the Isola Bella, with a gondola for the lake. The Isola Bella stayed on the drawing board but proof of the gondola and gondolier can be seen in a painting done by E. Adveno Brooke in 1859. At Bowood a local parson felt in the garden 'that I ought to have a copy of Dante in my hand or a volume of the Sonnets of Petrarch'.

The basic ingredients of an Italian garden were a balustraded terrace; sculpture; gravel and some vertical accents from topiary or cypresses. Portugal laurels, grown as standards, were acceptable substitutes for orange trees and often there were fountains.

Houses of any substance were pinned down by one terrace and sometimes more. Flat level areas of very cultivated garden descended, as at Shrublands, to the view of Suffolk countryside beyond. Views out from the house were important and the transition from art to nature was abrupt. The vistas were enormous. At Chatsworth, Paxton mixed wild with formal indiscriminately, causing a contemporary critic to observe that 'the combination of forest trees, wild undergrowth and brilliant flowers – art and nature thus bringing together gaiety and sombreness, order and wildness – all this is in my opinion, opposed to the dictates of good taste.'

In order to do justice to the head gardeners' talents the parterres in these historical gardens tended to be more influenced by Versailles than Vignola. The bedding plants which filled the parterres came increasingly to have a pattern of their own. Carpet bedding used foliage plants all of the same height – often these were succulents – to create geometrical patterns or, later, pictorial emblems: monograms and heraldic emblems were the most discreet uses to which this new device was put. The butterflies, which appeared in the gardens of the Crystal Palace in 1875, suggested that portraits of anything were possible. The new plants grown for their leaves were much more amenable to this craft than flowers; they could be sheered over to keep them all the same height and their contrasting foliage provided more variety and impact than flowers could. Some pelargoniums, like the

The new Fernery at Kingston Lacy in Dorset is on the site of an old fern garden. These specialist areas were particular favourites with the mid-Victorians who had a craze for collecting exotic forms of fern, which they often grew in the rockery.

Pages 140–141: Red geraniums in urns on a wall were a traditional feature in Victorian gardens. At Flintham they flank the steps from the terrace, on either side of the characteristically wide view.

Opposite: Ferns are not difficult to grow in moist soil and shade but there are only a few which will put up with dry conditions, such as the Hart's tongue fern and the common polypody.

143

The giant tree ferns at Penjerrick in Cornwall have all the qualities most prized by the Victorians, who loved vegetable monsters, ferns and anything exotic from faraway places. They thrive in the warmer, damper areas of the British Isles.

145

The Victorians, who liked everything on the grand scale, were particularly fond of ferns and tropical plants, so the giant tree ferns at Trengwainton would have given them enormous pleasure. Dicksonia antartica *grows wild in New Zealand and is not hardy in the British Isles, except in very favoured places.*

tri-coloured 'Crystal Palace Gem' were included in the carpet bedding, but not allowed to flower.

The beauty of leaves was also something which the Victorians favoured in the shrubbery and the park. Trees like the copper beech and the purple *Prunus pissardii* were highly prized, and gold, silver and variegated shrubs and plants were also popular. For ferns there was a craze. 'The ferns, though flowerless, are the most graceful and beautiful of their lower world ... when they are perched on the tiny islets of a gently murmuring stream, they are the still feature of crowning beauty as their waving fronds move responsively to the breeze and kiss with their delicate lips the tumbling water, as if caressing the element which ministers to the most vital principle of their existence.' The author of these words wrote several books on fern culture. He was not alone in his expertise. Fern collecting was another pastime suitable for ladies and, where there was no room to set aside a special place for ferns, they often took over the rockery. Some ferns could only be grown indoors in the miniature glasshouses known as Wardian cases. The rare, filmy fern from Tonbridge Wells was a favourite parlour plant, which was so much collected that it almost became extinct.

Conifers, which show some of the same qualities as ferns on a grand scale, also became a cult and no garden was complete without a selection of exotic evergreens. Many

of these, like the Monterey pine and the Sitka spruce, had been sent back to England by the plant collector David Douglas in the 1820s and 1830s. 'You will begin to think that I manufacture Pines at my pleasure,' he wrote in a letter to Kew. But the conifer that was planted in any garden of note was the Wellingtonia, which Messrs Veitch started selling in the summer of 1854, for two guineas a tree. The Victorian passion for natural wonders was thoroughly gratified by the giant redwood from California and they planted it everywhere. *The Gardener's Chronicle* carried an article by another collector Cobb describing the Wellingtonias which he had seen on his last plant hunting trip. 'A tree recently felled measured about 300 feet in length with a diameter, including bark, 29 feet 2 inches at 5 feet from the ground ... Of this vegetable monster, 21 feet of the bark, from the lower part of the trunk, have been put in the natural form in San Francisco for exhibition; it there forms a spacious carpeted room, and contains a piano, with seats for 40 persons. On one occasion 140 children were admitted without inconvenience.'

The other evergreen which gave a garden status was the Monkey Puzzle. This was perhaps more suitable for smaller establishments where it occupied pride of place in the front garden and occasionally it appeared (as at Biddulph in Staffordshire) in the role of a centre piece for a bedding scheme. In larger landscapes, woods were interspersed with several varieties of conifers and avenues of these trees also began to appear in the park or to

Glendurgan is the perfect place for a collection of exotic plants. The waterside plant Gunnera (manicata) *was introduced from Brazil in 1867. Its leaves unfurl into huge umbrellas eight foot tall and six foot wide. 'I believe the great secret for ensuring its reaching gigantic proportions is to feed the brute', wrote E. A. Bowles, the early twentieth-century plantsman.*

Ferns have a long association with stonework. The Victorians often grew them rather unsuitably on rockeries where they must have occasionally found conditions rather dry. At Newby Hall old habits die hard and ferns are associated with various pieces of masonry in a happier setting than they might have occupied a hundred years ago.

mark a drive. The restrained plantings of Kent and Brown, who had used almost entirely native varieties, were soon adorned with large numbers of foreign trees and shrubs. Waves of ponticum rhododendrons were encouraged to lap around the trees in the woodland, while nearer to the house collections of new rhododendron cultivars were assembled. The appetite for foreign plants was insatiable; if the layout of the garden provided instruction in history, its contents amounted to a geography lesson.

Nowhere was geography so well illustrated as at Biddulph, where fourteen acres were divided into different areas to represent particular countries or places. James Bateman, who made the garden in the 1840s, had a passion for plant collecting. With the help of his friend Edward Cook, who was a man of many talents, he laid out a series of enclosed gardens to provide suitable conditions for the rare plants which he wanted to grow. Bateman's wife Maria had connections with the leading nursery firm of Loddidges who supplied many things for the garden. Plants which Sir Joseph Hooker collected in the Himalayas appeared at Biddulph, as did introductions from the Far East, brought back by the Scottish Robert Fortune. There was the statutory Italian garden, an avenue of Wellingtonias and a fernery and a pinetum, which might all have been found in gardens of a similar size at that date, but Bateman's botanical treasure trove was unique and its setting still stands to amaze the twentieth-century visitor. In one place gigantic rock work was

Naturalized exotics were a feature of nineteenth-century gardens. The skunk cabbage and gunnera by the water at Heale House in Wiltshire are strange enough for Victorian tastes.

Opposite: The conservatory at Flintham was built by Thomas Hine in 1853. It is tall enough to house fully grown mimosa trees, which can be viewed at eye level from the Italianate balcony.

Waves of ponticum rhododendrons rolled through woodland in the last century, but the newer, brighter cultivars were scarce enough to be reserved for the areas around the house. At High Beeches in Sussex today there is no shortage of colour to place further afield.

designed by Cook to represent the Great Wall of China which curled round a corner of fabulous Cathay. Oriental plants grew round a Chinese pool and there was a Chinese temple. The Chinese bridge, dragon parterre and willow pattern palimpsest were all fantastical elements which brought to life Chambers' eighteenth-century descriptions of Chinese gardens. In another part of the garden, visitors were led through a timbered Cheshire cottage to find they were standing in an Egyptian court, complete with sphinxes and a pyramid of yew. This dramatic garden still conveys the excitement which the Victorians must have felt when they came to admire that 'suitable home for nearly all the hardy members of that great plant family, which the curiosity or taste of man has discovered or cultivated'.

Many of the trees and shrubs planted by Batemen still exist; it is the smaller exotic plants which have disappeared from this and other Victorian gardens. Among those plants which were most popular with all gardeners were verbenas from Uruguay, water lilies from India, lobelias and dahlias from Mexico, chrysanthemums from China and orchids from the South American rainforests, while mignonette from Egypt was frequently grown in the front gardens of suburban streets. With the invention of the Wardian case there was no limit to the number of plants which could survive the long sea voyage from the other side of the world. After 1830, the sealed glass case invented by Ward was extensively used

to prevent imported plants and cuttings from drying out, but the new rare plants were expensive and tended to appear in aristocratic gardens for a decade before reaching a wider public. In 1829 the dahlia was recorded by Thomas Hogg as 'the most fashionable flower in this country,' yet it was not until much later that its exotic flowers began to appear in smaller gardens.

Small gardens continued to act as repositories for all the unfashionable flowers which had made way for the new exotics and also for those displaced by industry. The florist's flowers, like pinks and auriculas, which had been cultivated by the weavers who worked at home, no longer thrived in the smoky factory towns, but were often found in country gardens. Mrs Gaskell describes the simplest sort of cottage garden near Manchester which contained, 'little more than "a few berry bushes", space for potatoes, onions and cabbages, as well as the odd herb; with a rose tree and some marigolds to flavour the salt beef broth', but George Eliot gives an account of a place that was better cherished in *Scenes of Clerical Life*. There there was 'a charming paradisaical mingling of all that was pleasant to the eye and good for food. The rich flower-border running along every walk, with its endless succession of spring flowers, anemones, auriculas, wall-flowers, sweet-williams, campanulas, snap-dragons, and tiger-lilies, had its taller beauties such as moss and Provence roses, varied with espalier apple-trees; the crimson of a carnation was carried out in the lurking

The appetite for foreign plants was insatiable. Leaves of ponticum rhododendrons lapped through the woodland, but nearer the house exotic species of azaleas like these at Leonardslee made for very colourful gardens.

After the invention of the Wardian case in 1830, the number of imported plants increased dramatically. The search for rarer, brighter flowers gathered momentum towards the end of the century. Nowhere were these collected so assiduously as in the Cornish gardens. At Glendurgan, which was laid out in the 1830s, rhododendrons and acid-loving plants have always been a speciality.

crimson of the neighbouring strawberry beds; you gathered a moss-rose one moment and a bunch of currants the next; you were in a delicious fluctuation between the scent of jasmine and the juice of gooseberries.'

In the gardens of trim Victorian villas abundance on such a scale was not a feature. The grass was well cut (since the invention of the lawn mower by Mr Budding in 1830 lawns were kept short and of an even length), and maintenance continued to be up to Loudon's exacting standards. The ceramic tiles which edged the flower beds and paths kept everything in its place and any stray plants which might once have seeded themselves in old-fashioned gravelled paths no longer found a hold in the asphalt which increasingly replaced gravel. Mass-produced cast-iron urns and concreted ponds added more hard surfaces to small gardens than in any previous age. The adornment of an aucuba, a monkey puzzle, or a variegated holly combined with a bed full of geraniums surrounding a standard rose made the average front garden a far cry from George Eliot's idyllic picture.

Yet there was a yearning for country life among the new generation of town people. By the end of the nineteenth century there were many more inhabitants of built-up areas than there were of the country, but these exiles from rural life often still had connections with the countryside, or memories of a time when they had lived there themselves. Townspeople made expeditions to watch haymaking and harvesting, or simply to enjoy the fresh air. A popular outing for factory workers was a day trip by railway to the country, or to visit the gardens of the rich, because the air of the cities was heavily polluted and unhealthy and gardening was not suited to the smoke. Nostalgia for what seemed to be a lost idyll was on the increase. After the 1880s, when agriculture suffered from cheap imports of American corn, many landowners were forced to sell and labourers gave up their rural lives to find work in factories: then dreaming about the country became endemic.

The Victorian artists who painted thatched cottages surrounded by poultry and girls in sunbonnets, among toppling hollyhocks and delphiniums, with roses round the window, all fuelled this dream. Artistic licence allowed them to paint more than they probably saw. In a watercolour by Arthur Claude Strachan, peonies, roses, tulips, delphiniums, poppies, daisies, pinks and lilies flower simultaneously. In Miss Jekyll's garden Helen Allingham painted plants which, according to Penelope Hobhouse, an authority on Miss Jekyll, do not appear on plans of the same border. In reality many of the gardens must have been more like Mrs Gaskell's memory of a cottage garden than George Eliot's description of a late eighteenth-century farm, but the painters knew what they were looking for and its rarity added to the romance.

Before the enclosure of open fields, cottagers had owned a few acres, enough perhaps to grow some crops and feed some livestock to supplement their low wages. Bad landlords – and there were many of them – made little provision for giving their tenants room to improve their lot. Edward Hyams, who wrote on the cottage garden, has pointed out that the Acts of Enclosure did attempt to make some provision for compensation for ancient rights in the form of garden allotments, but that few cottagers benefited from this. Between 1845 and 1867 half a million acres of land were enclosed, but out of this only 2000 were reserved for allotments. Poverty and homelessness forced many of those dispossessed of their livelihood to look for work in towns. Those that remained in the country, even when supported by philanthropic landlords, were often too poor to spare much space for ornamentals and in order to stop the drift of labour away from the land, competitions were organized for vegetable growing. As Brent Elliott, the authority on Victorian gardens, points out, some landowners insisted on flower gardens to improve the look of estate villages but the majority of cottage gardens were as they had always been, places for growing vegetables and fruit, with a few pot herbs and the odd rose bush (often 'Maiden's Blush') or honeysuckle against the house.

Many of the flowers which were grown still had a medicinal role. The leaves of honeysuckle were boiled to make a healing oil for coughs or nerves. Damask rose petals made a purging syrup; eglantine preserved the hair, jasmine flower oil made a liniment; pansies were good for convulsions and hollyhocks among other things cured swollen gums and killed worms. Sweet rocket, wallflowers, lupins, irises, foxgloves, mullein, lavender and countless other 'cottage' plants were traditional remedies for everyday ills. 'Cottage gardening, like cottage life, is mispresented by authors unacquainted with the subject, who deal in fine writing and take one-sided views and give the thing a sentimental dash for the sake of effect. When we read of the allotment gardens near Nottingham being rich in the choicest kind of roses, we mistake the thing altogether; for the capital embarked in such gardens is a clear proof that the owner is a man of some substance,' wrote a contributor to *The Gardener's Chronicle* in 1872. Poverty-stricken tenants had no money for ornamental gardening: the pig, the chickens and the vegetable patch were essential; flowers were not. But the fashionable view of cottage life was romantic to the point of sentimentality. Dickens describes the reaction to a little watercolour sketch of a cottage in a London drawing room. '"Lovely! What a dear old place!" said the guests. "It makes one quite enamoured of the country," exclaimed Lady Fanshawe, one of the most determined diners out in Mayfair. "I never look at a scene like that without wishing I could give up London altogether ... It would be so charming to get rid of conventionality and be perfectly natural."'

Above: Peonies are traditional cottage plants which have been refined and hybridized by the plant breeders. Their beauty is short lived, but their leaves deserve a place in the garden in their own right. In species peonies the seed pods are an added attraction.

The new generation of townspeople yearned for country life and the myth of the cottage garden was a constant theme in novels and watercolours of the period. In reality, most cottages needed every inch of ground for growing food: flowers were a luxury. Gardens like this very pretty traditional plot in East Anglia were often painted, but were perhaps not as numerous as they are generally supposed to have been.

157

Many of the cottage flowers, like those in this East Anglian cottage garden, were grown for their medicinal value. The leaves of honeysuckle were boiled for coughs; roses, lupins, foxgloves, lavender and countless other 'cottage' plants were remedies for minor ills.

If genuine cottage gardens were rare in the middle decades of the century, old-fashioned flower borders were not. Donald Beaton, the head gardener at Shrublands who contributed to *The Cottage Gardener* magazine in the middle of the century, regularly wrote about the difficulties of managing the mixed border. There were examples of picturesque borders and topiary at Arley Hall in Cheshire from 1846. Plans for the flower borders of hardy plants with hollyhocks, sunflowers, lupins and snapdragons are still in existence today and the flower beds, which Miss Jekyll admired, are virtually unchanged. In the gardens of rectories, manor houses and farms the borders of perennials which Shirley Hibberd recommended in addition to bedding out could also be seen. Generally the front of the house was reserved for bedding plants, while to the side lay borders of perennials. A painting of John Atkinson Grimshaw's own garden near Leeds clearly shows this arrangement – which Hibberd favoured.

According to Canon Ellacombe, writing in the 1890s, 'the parsonage garden some years ago was a home for hundreds of good old-fashioned flowers, but I am afraid no gardens suffered more from the bedding craze, which swept them clear of all their own long cherished beauties and reduced them to the dull level of uniformity with their neighbours gardens, or to miniature mockeries of Trentham or Cliveden.' Canon Ellacombe's own garden was full of old-fashioned beauties. He wrote about them often in

The Guardian and described cyclamen, hellebores, asters, anemones, dogtooth violets, irises, roses, lilies, peonies, crown imperials, wallflowers, sunflowers and many other plants which had been banished from bedding schemes. He used bedding plants like heliotropes, geraniums, calceolarias and begonias as single plants to fill gaps in his borders but did not like them massed. The early cottage gardens tracked down by the watercolour artists or described in the literature of the period owed more to the taste of the squire and the parson than to that of the farm labourer. Canon Ellacombe and other country parsons like him gave cuttings and plants to their parishioners; a good landlord often did the same. 'Our curate is not only a lover of flowers himself, but a zealous missionary florist. He was instrumental in establishing our Cottage-Gardening Society, which has reclaimed many a waste place from sterility, many a sot from the beerhouse, and brought comfort to many a home,' wrote Dean Hole in the 1880s. At Harlaxton Manor in Lincolnshire the head gardener supervised all the gardens in the estate village and where cottage gardens were encouraged, perennial plants made more economic sense than expensive bedding varieties.

Less *bona fide* cottagers like the educated, but impoverished, Miss Mitford created what we now think of as a traditional cottage garden. She lived in 'a miniature house, with many additions, little odds and ends of places, pantries and what not, all angles and of a charming in-and-outness'; hollyhocks, roses and honeysuckles grew against the walls of

At Arley Hall in Cheshire there were mixed flower borders and topiary from 1846. These were some of the earliest examples of the revival of interest in old-fashioned gardens. The flowerbeds which Miss Jekyll admired are almost unchanged today. Hollyhocks, snapdragons, sunflowers and lupins are all shown on early plans of these borders.

the house and the little garden behind was full of 'common flowers, tulips, pinks, larkspurs, peonies, stocks and carnations with an arbour of privet, where one lives in a delicious green light and looks out on the gayest of all gay flower-beds'. Miss Mitford's village was spruce and pretty; her descriptions of village life which first appeared in *The Lady's Magazine* from 1824 were so popular that they were reprinted and re-read throughout the century.

The 'cottage garden' had an enormous amount of publicity from writers and artists during the Victorian age. They could be said to have created a climate in its favour. The pre-Raphaelites made no secret of the fact that they hated parterre plants. William Morris called carpet bedding 'an aberration of the human mind'. The aesthetes were prone to walking about with lilies or chose, like Oscar Wilde, to be 'the first to devote my subtle brain chords to the worship of the sunflower'. Ruskin persuaded a band of undergraduates, including Oscar Wilde, to rise at dawn and help him turn the boggy ground at North Hinksey into a country road bordered with wild flowers. He did not suggest that they made gardens. Even politicians took up the cause. 'How I hate modern gardens,' says Disraeli's St Aldegonde in *Lothair*, speaking as he looks out of the window. 'What a horrid thing this is! One might as well have a mosaic pavement there. Give me cabbage roses, sweet peas and wallflowers. That is my idea of a garden. Corisande's garden is the only sensible thing of the sort.' Corisande's garden was a painter's dream with 'huge bushes of honeysuckle and bowers of sweet pea and Jassamine clustering over the walls and gilly flowers scenting with their sweet breath the ancient bricks from which they seemed to spring. There were banks of violets which the southern breeze always stirred and mignonette filled every vacant nook. As they entered now it seemed a blaze of roses and carnations, though one recognized in a moment the presence of the lily, the heliotrope and the stock.' Such formidable apostles of old-fashioned gardens did not go unheard.

Well-grown turk's cap lilies at Wallington in Northumberland lean across the path. Lilies were a favourite with the Arts and Crafts Movement and aesthetes were prone to carrying them around. There is, however, nothing dilettante about growing lilies, for most of them demand moist soil and perfect drainage, which are never the easiest conditions to supply.

Opposite: This winding cottage garden path would have delighted Helen Allingham, whose watercolours often included some imaginative out-of-season flowers to give the borders the abundance which she loved. This well-managed garden is near Bressingham in Norfolk.

161

CHAPTER 7

BRIAR ROSES, LILIES, TOPIARY & BORDERS

*'I like everything old fashioned. Old fashioned things are
so much the honestest'*

A Summer Herbaceous Border *by Lillian Stannard (1877–1944)*

THE GARDENS WHICH WERE MOST TALKED ABOUT IN THE
eighteenth century were those made by the landed gentry; in the
nineteenth, attention was focused on the work of professional gardeners;
but by the twentieth century the age of the home-owning amateur had
arrived. The Victorian worship of home life and family values raised
domesticity from a moral virtue to a divine calling: keeping a house and a
garden in good order was, according to Ruskin, a high vocation. Articles and books
about interior decoration began to appear in the last quarter of the century with titles
like *A Place for Art in the House*, *Hints on Household Taste* and *Beautiful Houses*, indicating
that what had once been the province of aesthetes and artists was becoming of interest
to a wider public.

Throughout most of Queen Victoria's reign moral fibre was rated higher than
taste. James Lees Milne remembers in his autobiography that his father's 'deadliest most
offensive adjective was "artistic". It denoted decadence, disloyalty to the Crown and unnatural vice.' The extreme dilettantism of *The Yellow Book* was still new enough to arouse
disapproval of this kind, but the sober traditional style of Morris and his followers, which
had seemed so revolutionary in its early days, was now much more acceptable. The Arts
and Crafts Movement aimed to leave its mark on every visible aspect of domestic life. It

*Opposite: Lovers of the picturesque lowered their
aspirations in the nineteenth century. Rustic work
was the result of too much exposure to the rocks and
banditti of Salvator Rosa's paintings. A hut in the
garden made from rough-hewn timbers was very
desirable. This one at Killerton in Devonshire has
patterns of fir cones on the inside walls.*

The pergolas and shady tunnels of earlier gardens were revived by followers of the Arts and Crafts Movement, who wanted to leave their mark on the garden as well as the house. At Heale House wooden posts rising from box hedges support iron hoops with roses and ivy.

emphasized rural traditions and the 'Olde Englishe' way of life which had existed before the Industrial Revolution. Nostalgia was a sentiment in which more people than artists could indulge. It was a long overdue reaction to the excesses of the age. Burne Jones claimed that in an age of sofas and cushions 'Newman taught me to be indifferent to comfort and in an age of materialism he taught me to venture all on the unseen.' The gardens which the pre-Raphaelites and their followers painted and created reflected these precepts. They were modest but ethereal. The enchantments of the Middle Ages, of briar roses, lilies and damsels, could all be present in a garden. The aesthetic movement, which included writers like Tennyson and Henry James and also embraced painters with the popular appeal of Helen Allingham, had as much to do with changing attitudes to gardens as the literary coterie of the eighteenth century had in their day. Ruskin's denunciation of greed, his views on conservation and his long campaign for aesthetic standards all had some bearing on the way in which people treated the space outside their houses. They began to feel uncomfortable about cheque-book horticulture, and they gloried in tradition, 'I like everything old fashioned,' says one of Trollope's heroines; 'Old fashioned things are so much the honestest.' William Morris' own gardens were very old-fashioned; they were simple, secret and romantic. There was an apple orchard at the Red House in Kent and at Kelmscott in Oxfordshire he grew raspberries on trellises. These gardens and those which

The vine-covered walk at Powis Castle is on the site of a demolished vinery. William Robinson preferred to use vines for 'garlanding copses', but Gertrude Jekyll thought that 'the best of all climbing plants whether for wall, arbour, or pergola, is undoubtedly the grape-vine'. The patches of bright yellow here are golden marjoram.

included similar features all suggested a return to earlier values. The presence of orchards, enclosed gardens, topiary, trellis and cobbled or brick paths instead of asphalt, combined with the plants grown in Elizabethan, or better still medieval, England, indicated a preference for the simple life and a respect for tradition. Such gardens were a stand against materialism and ugliness. Old English names were preferred to botanical Latin and early gardening manuals were consulted in the search for a lost past. 'If there be a chance for a filbert walk seize it,' wrote one authority. Bacon's essay *Of Gardens* was an important source of ideas, as was William Lawson's *A New Orchard and Garden* which had first been published in 1618.

The early Arts and Crafts gardens were cut off from the landscape; they were domestic and provided a setting for the house and their scale was human and unostentatious. They were in direct contrast to the display gardens of the preceding generation. Their enclosures were hedged with yew or creeper-clad walls, which shut out the view. The gardens that were most admired and painted were full of green architecture which had grown to a comfortable size. The topiary and hedges planted during the revival of 'period' gardens earlier in the century had billowed into huge romantic shapes by the 1880s. At places like Packwood, Levens, Chastleton and Arley it was hard not to believe that the yews were planted before the landscape movement. Most people believed that any

*Topiary was much admired at the turn of the
nineteenth century. The fat bulges of yew at Great
Dixter were planted and trained by Nathaniel
Lloyd (the father of Christopher Lloyd, the well-
known gardener). Topiary frames of heavy wire are
now being manufactured, which indicates a revival
of interest in a style of gardening which had a long
period of unpopularity earlier this century.*

garden which contained mature hedges and topiary must be at least two centuries old, whereas often they had been planted not much more than fifty years ago. There were also some misconceptions about 'early' plants, which later knowledge suggests may not have been quite as early as late nineteenth-century historians assumed. The period garden revivalists towards the end of Queen Victoria's reign did not want modern plants in their gardens as the earlier revivalists had done, which made for much more restrained plantings. A little gentle colour throughout the year, rather than a summer blast of red, blue and yellow was now the aim. Too much clutter indoors and too much ostentation outside had led to a new taste for refinement and modesty. 'The modern millionaire's made-by-contract, opulent style of gardening,' which gave the plantsman E.A. Bowles 'a sort of gardening bilious attack and a feeling of pity for the plants and contempt for the gardening skill that relies upon Bank of England notes for manure' was on its way out. Those who may not have absorbed the whole of the Arts and Crafts philosophy were dissatisfied with gardens which were bare for so many months of the year and a groundswell of opinion was growing against bedding out.

The voice which was heard above all others, decrying unnatural practices and the destruction of old plants, was later to claim most of the credit for the revolution in taste. William Robinson was described after his death as the 'grand old man of the new gardening'. His reaction to the horticultural excesses of the day advocated less of a return to history than the aesthetes proposed, for he rejected rigid formality in favour of natural beauty. He allowed simple formal flower beds near the house for botanical treasures, but would only praise design where it reinforced 'the site, soil, climate and labours' of a garden. The plant was to come first, and not the architecture. His record for publicizing the return to nature was unsurpassed, but much of what he said so loudly was also said by others, often in his own publications, which in later editions appeared as all his own work.

William Robinson was an Irishman who came to England at the age of twenty-three He found work at Regent's Park, where he was put in charge of the herbaceous plants, which included a collection of native flowers. He was quickly recognized as a brilliant botanist when he started to write about plants. By the age of thirty-five he had written seven books. In the best tradition of the Victorian head gardener he started a weekly gardening magazine. In 1883 his most important work *The English Flower Garden* was published, which was a compilation of writing by many contributors. Gertrude Jekyll, Canon Ellacombe and Dean Hole all wrote sections of the book, which Robinson revised many times, but in later editions there is no indication that anyone other than Robinson was responsible for this massive polemic. He was a skilled and impassioned crusader and the legacy of his campaign can be seen today in all those gardens where daffodils are naturalized; in wild flower meadows, with cut grass paths, in mixed borders and woodland gardens, and wherever roses rampage through trees or appear with other flowers.

Robinson and his team had the support of Ruskin and Morris; Morris's remarks on carpet bedding (which made him blush with shame) were quoted at the front of each edition of *The Flower Garden*. Robinson shared the Arts and Crafts taste for simple single flowers and informal planting, but while their concern was purely visual and historical, Robinson with his botanical training concentrated on the needs of the plants, aiming to display the greatest number of these in the simplest way. He had no overall plan for his own garden, which he made at Gravetye in Sussex, but took trouble to place each plant carefully, often grouping them as they would be seen in nature. Wild flowers were naturalized in fields under hedgerows, and sometimes allowed into the garden. The pretty but invasive speedwell and the insuppressible oxalis were both encouraged by Robinson, wild flowers he described as 'Nature's own wild self' and he far preferred them to exotics. He liked a grey or green background which was in accordance with Arts and Crafts greenery-yallery taste, but he was not fond of topiary or the hard lines of evergreen hedges,

Opposite: The yew maze at Somerleyton Hall in Suffolk is another example of the manifestation of the Olde Worlde-ism favoured by the Arts and Crafts Movement, who seized every opportunity to recreate the past. The clipping involved here is phenomenal.

Above: The alpine meadow at Wisley would have been Robinson's dream. Here Narcissus bulbocodium, *the tiny damp-loving wild daffodil, has naturalized and spread to make a carpet of yellow in the grass.*

Drifts of daffodils in the grass were made popular by William Robinson, who suggested that 'grouping and scattering these in a natural and pretty way required care because the tendency of men was to plant in stiff and set or too regular masses'. Robinson's art is well practised at Cotehele in Devon.

171

The woodland, or wild, garden was developed by Robinson at the beginning of this century. Azaleas interspersed with wild hyacinths, red campion, forget-me-nots, globe flowers, columbines, primroses, cowslips, campanulas and golden rods were recommended. At Leonardslee in Sussex the ground cover is now more foliage than flowers.

which Morris and his followers admired for their ancient traditional virtues.

Robinson's favourite painter was Corot, whose full-blown windswept trees were very much to his liking. (He also admired Crome and Turner). Flowering trees in grass; lilacs, laburnums and hawthorns were all a mark of a Robinsonian garden, as were wide drifts of one species; plants for damp places; and plenty of ground cover. The 'new' gardening banned naked earth and preferred to see something like comfrey, Solomon's seal or the dwarf partridge berry (*Leycesteria*) under shrubs. Under roses, pansies, pinks, gypsophila and the 'Narbon flax' were recommended and manure was abhorred. 'Instead of mulching the beds in the usual way and always vexing the surface with attentions I thought needless, we covered them with pansies, violets, stonecrops, rockfoils, thymes and any little rock plants to spare ... It seems to me that to cover beds near the house with excreta from the farm is anything but a sanitary or necessary thing to do. We never mulch the beds but cover them with beautiful plants instead.' Instead of being banished to a separate garden, the roses grown at Gravetye were reinstated as 'the queen of the flower garden'. They were trained up 'rough yew stakes' and they were raised wherever possible from cuttings rather than being grafted on to the wild rose as was the normal practice of the day.

This new way of gardening which left plants to grow naturally and loosened the trim hold of Victorian maintenance was much easier to manage than bedding out had been. It

was also cheaper. This suited the suburban gardeners with small plots who could not afford to pay full-time gardeners or to heat acres of glass for bedding plants. Increasingly work in the garden was organized by the woman in the house and at the turn of the century there were several female authorities connected with gardening. In 1895 women started working at Kew and various horticultural colleges soon began to offer training for girls. Lady Wolseley founded a College for Lady Gardeners at Glynde and during the 1914 War, women gardeners came into their own when they were left in charge while the men went off to fight. Mrs Ewing, the children's writer, had formed the Parkinson Society which was dedicated to the preservation of old garden plants. Mrs Earle wrote a series of gardening books, of which the most famous was *Pot Pourri from a Surrey Garden* and she too was attracted by old-fashioned flowers. She recalled the garden of her childhood where double white rockets and Oriental poppies grew 'which had peculiar charms for us, because although we hardly realized it, such gardens were already beginning to grow out of fashion, sacrificed to the new bedding out system, which altered the whole gardening of Europe'. Mrs Earle was practical enough to know 'that "wild gardening" as a synonym for leaving alone, spells failure and deterioration for everything, even the common primroses,' and she admitted that the general effect of her garden was often 'crowded, spotty and untidy', but her aim was 'to grow as many plants as possible the whole year round'.

The water garden was another wild area which Edwardian gardeners loved. Gertrude Jekyll preferred to plant on the banks of a small stream like this one at Trengwainton in Cornwall 'where there is a happy prospect of delightful ways of arranging and enjoying the beautiful plants that we love'. Celandines and kingcups, like those seen here, were particular favourites.

173

Above: In dry gardens the erythroniums, or dog's tooth violets, do better in damp places. They are good candidates for shade and their lush leaves look good near water.

Rockeries were notoriously artificial places. Miss Jekyll did not favour a shockingly sudden rock garden 'but a gradual unfolding valley where everything falls into its place'. This boulder-strewn pool with ferns at Newby Hall would not suit the sort of alpines associated with a real rockery, but its arrangement would have pleased the 'wild' gardeners.

174

*Claude Monet's garden at Giverny was a great
inspiration to Gertrude Jekyll. This Chinese bridge
and weeping willow at Heale House provides a
modern gloss on a well-known theme.*

Lutyens laid out the garden at Ammerdown in Somerset in characteristically architectural fashion, even though he had to twist an axis or two. Modern bedding now fills the box-edged beds.

Miss Willmott was a prodigal gardener who employed 103 gardeners in her three gardens in England, Italy and France. Many good garden plants today bear her name, or that of her garden at Warley in Essex, and gardeners still plant bulbs for naturalizing in the way which she recommended, by throwing them on to the ground and digging them in where they fall. Her seed lists were sent to botanists all over the world, for she grew enormous varieties of rare plants. Gertrude Jekyll, whose friend she was, called Miss Willmott 'the greatest of living women-gardeners'. All of these women were gifted amateurs who achieved professional standards in the gardens which they made.

Gertrude Jekyll has outlasted her friend Ellen Willmott to become a name which is famous even to those who care very little about gardening. Like Repton in his day, Jekyll picked out the best elements from the confused ideals of her age and gave them a balance and unity which was much needed at the time. Just as Repton stood between factions warring about the role of art and nature in the garden, so Jekyll found herself surrounded by controversy. Robinson was raging against the role of the architect in the garden and, in particular, that new hybrid the landscape architect; '.. a stupid term of French origin implying the union of two distinct studies, one dealing with varied life in a thousand different kinds and the natural beauty of the earth and the other with stones and bricks and their putting together. The training for either of these arts is wide apart from the training

At Hestercombe in Somerset Lutyens set a lily pond in radials of paving. The variety of materials he used made even large expanses of stonework easy on the eye. If all this had been flagstones it would be a very dank area.

demanded for the other, and the earnest practice of the one leaves no time, even if there were the genius, for the other.' The first President of the Institute of Landscape Architects was Thomas Mawson, an Arts and Crafts garden architect, whose work was rather different from Robinson's. He modelled his designs on those of Repton and blamed Capability Brown for destroying the 'very root foundations of his art'. The chief protagonist for Mawson's ordered style of gardening was Sir Reginald Blomfield, an architect who thought that gardens should be an extension of the architecture of the house, governed by the same principles of design as the building. Sir Reginald wrote an elegant book in praise of *The Formal Garden in England*, which attacked Robinson and his followers for their lack of principles and their indiscriminate abuse of formal gardening; 'after which they incontinently drop the question of garden design and go off at a tangent on horticulture and hothouses. A great deal is said about nature and her beauty and fidelity to nature and so on; but as the landscape gardener never takes the trouble to state precisely what he means by nature and indeed prefers to use the word in half a dozen different senses, we are not very much the wiser, so far as principles are concerned.'

His book included a history of garden design and showed how modern gardens might contain examples of trellis, knots, espalier work, topiary and sculpture. Like the Arts and Crafts gardeners, Blomfield drew heavily on the examples of the seventeenth-century

The garden at Hestercombe was laid out by Lutyens and planted by Jekyll. It has now been beautifully restored and is the headquarters of the Somerset Fire Brigade.

Opposite: Harold Peto was one of the devotees of the picturesque formal garden. From his Italian travels he brought home statues to his garden at Iford Manor in Wiltshire.

writers William Lawson and Gervase Markham but the gardens with which he was concerned tended to be on the grand scale. Neither Robinson nor Blomfield would give an inch of ground in their argument. What was needed was someone who could see both points of view, who could anchor a house to its setting, but in doing so could make the garden feel like a part of the landscape. The qualities of architect and gardener had been successfully combined in Repton but the problem was solved even more satisfactorily at the close of the nineteenth century by the striking of a partnership between a middle-aged gardener and a young architect.

Gertrude Jekyll was sensible enough to see that her practical and artistic skills would look better framed and presented by an architect; her partnership with the young Edwin Lutyens brought unity to the Robinson-Blomfield dichotomy. Miss Jekyll was firstly an artist and secondly a plantswoman. She spent her youth copying Turners in the National Gallery and she appreciated Impressionist painting. She had in her time tried metalwork, embroidery and carving; she knew and admired Ruskin and Morris and shared with them a respect for tradition and a sense of beauty. In gardening, she found the perfect combination of Art and Craft.

> I am strongly of the opinion that the possession of a quantity of plants, however good the plants may be themselves and however ample their number, does not make a garden; it only makes a *collection*. Having got the plants, the great thing is to use them with careful selection and definite intention. Merely having them, or having them planted unassorted in garden spaces, is only like having a box of paints from the best colourman, or, to go one step further, it is like having portions of these paints set out upon a palette. This does not constitute a picture; and it seems to me that the duty we owe to our gardens and to our own bettering in our gardens is so to use the plants that they shall form beautiful pictures; and that, while delighting our eyes they should be always training those eyes to a more exalted criticism; to a state of mind and artistic conscience that will not tolerate bad or careless combination or any sort of misuse of plants, but in which it becomes a point of honour to be always striving for the best.

Gertrude Jekyll wrote for Robinson's magazine and contributed to *The Flower Garden*, but although she referred to him as 'a strong champion', she did not entirely share his philosophy. Gardens for her were more than the sum of the plants which they contained. Lutyens was only twenty when they met in 1889 but, with him, she developed a style of gardening which was far from Robinsonian and which lasted to become an inspiration to more than her own generation. The outdoor rooms which Lutyens arranged round a dominant architectural feature – a flight of steps, or a doorway or a pool perhaps – were designed to be furnished with plants. The plantings which Gertrude Jekyll added were rich and abundant. They provided the ornament for the architecture; a Lutyens garden seen without its Jekyll contribution can look hard and bare. Their formula was so successful that they made over a hundred gardens together. A similar synthesis combining architecture and horticulture, dispensed with an artist's flair, was later to be practised at Sissinghurst in Kent by Harold Nicolson and Vita Sackville-West.

Gertrude Jekyll never recommended a plant which she had not grown herself. Her

William Waldorf Astor, the early American tycoon, collected statuary for his Italian garden at Hever Castle while he lived in Rome. He created a special corner for his homage to Italy, out of sight of Anne Boleyn's castle, in a formal grass court, surrounded by high walls. At the end of his sculpture walk a loggia with a piazza looks out over an English lake.

Harold Peto was an architect with an Arts and Crafts background who, like many others of his day, fell in love with Italy. His garden at Iford Manor was an architectural lumber room of treasures picked up on his travels. The writer Christopher Hussey described Peto's style of gardening as picturesque-formal.

185

The Victorians did not underplant their roses but covered the ground instead with quantities of manure. This was a habit which William Robinson deplored. The campanulas which Graham Stuart Thomas has so successfully arranged between the roses at Mottisfont are in the approved Robinsonian style.

practical experience of gardening was formidable and in her observation of the way plants grew and looked she missed nothing. Describing an *Iris pallida dalmatica* she devotes two paragraphs to its colour and habit, ending up with 'an opal without any fire ... a pale bluish lilac as pale as a basin of starch and just transparent enough to show a trace of the orange portion of the beard. Aha, now I've got it – they are like a delicious plover's egg just shelled and ready to eat.' Colour was her speciality and she was not afraid to use it. She was the first to restrict borders to a limited range of colours, at her own garden at Munstead Wood in Surrey where she had built a functional, vernacular house for herself which was designed by Lutyens. She had a small grey garden but 'I badly want others and especially a gold garden, a blue garden and a green garden', she wrote. From her watercolour plans it is still possible to see exactly how she tackled a colour scheme.

In a sketch for a blue garden, long lozenges of delphiniums, *Clematis heracleifolia*, felicias, salvias, ceratostigmas and other blue flowering plants are interspersed with shafts of yellow. Miss Jekyll knew the value of contrast to enhance her chosen colour, so verbascums, lilies and white tree lupins highlighted the blue throughout the border. She also relied on strong architectural plants everywhere. Yew hedges, crambes, yuccas, rues, hostas, bergenias, choisyas and *Aruncus sylvester* all made a cool foil for colour. In mixed colour borders she would fade an impressionist haze into pale greys and misty blues, after

running through the spectrum of purple, crimson and sunset orange. At Munstead Wood the borders were very large indeed, but Gertrude Jekyll often designed for small gardens where she brought the same attention to detail. Her experience of handling herbaceous plants, both in her own and other people's gardens, was acquired over forty years. Her technique with mixed and herbaceous borders still influences garden making today. The role of the gardener she thought was to be 'always watching, noting, doing and putting oneself meanwhile into closest acquaintance and sympathy with growing things . . . As the critical faculty becomes keener, so does the standard of aim rise higher; and year by year the desired point seems always to elude attainment.'

Gertrude Jekyll worked very hard at creating beauty, for her it was a craft and not an accident. She always tried to compose her plants into pictures and planned something to look at for each month of the year so that different areas of the garden came into their own at different seasons, but the transition from one part of the garden to another had to be effortless, without 'any jarring obstruction'. The rock garden probably presented the greatest challenge; it had never sat at ease under English skies. Jane Loudon had admired rockeries for being a 'striking object in the landscape', but it was clear that the element of surprise had gone too far when a model of the Matterhorn, complete with Chamois, appeared in a garden near Henley on Thames. Robinson went over the top in his criticism

Many shrub roses, like this Nevada at Flintham, are modern hybrids, but the habit of growing them as loose bushes or allowing them to climb up trees was pioneered by William Robinson and Gertrude Jekyll.

Overleaf: Growing plants in paving stones is a luxury which the Edwardians could afford. The need for constant renewal of plants like the Dianthus seen here at Oare House makes this a rare sight. Weedkillers or cement keep most terraces free of flowers as well as weeds in modern labour-less gardens.

187

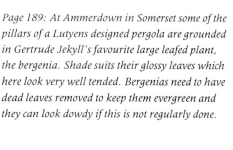

Page 189: At Ammerdown in Somerset some of the pillars of a Lutyens designed pergola are grounded in Gertrude Jekyll's favourite large leafed plant, the bergenia. Shade suits their glossy leaves which here look very well tended. Bergenias need to have dead leaves removed to keep them evergreen and they can look dowdy if this is not regularly done.

The double borders which line the kitchen garden at Helmingham Hall in Suffolk are packed with the sort of old-fashioned flowers which Gertrude Jekyll recommended for cutting and for beautifying the walled garden.

191

'Cottage' plants like foxgloves and love-in-a-mist jostle among rarer herbaceous perennials at Hatfield, and grass, not gravel, forms the paths. The abundance of this garden would have seemed very familiar to visitors before the First World War.

Opposite: 'A fine lesson and example is a wood of wild bluebells in May. It shows the value of doing one thing at a time and doing it largely and thoroughly well,' wrote Gertrude Jekyll. She would have approved of these bluebells at Bowood in Wiltshire.

of 'such ridiculous objects' where 'plants could not do otherwise than lead a sickly existence'. Miss Jekyll (although she did confess to admiring Sir Frank Crisp's Matterhorn) did not favour 'a shockingly sudden rock garden' but a 'gradual unfolding valley where everything falls into its place and a quiet progress through any one of the paths prevents a succession of garden pictures that look not so much as if they had been designed and made, but as if they had just happened to come so.' Often she found a terrace wall would serve just as well as a rockery for the alpine plants which were such a feature of the spring.

A home for moisture-loving plants could also be difficult to integrate. A Lutyens tank with water lilies often featured in his designs, but Gertrude Jekyll obviously preferred to plant on the banks of a small stream, 'where there was a happy prospect of delightful ways of arranging and enjoying the beautiful plants that we love'. At the edges of the gardens which she made with Lutyens, where the architecture lost its firm hold and the land shaded into woodland or wild places, Miss Jekyll exercised the same painstaking process of composition as she used everywhere else. She softened the fringes of woods with ferns, used bergenias or hostas at the edges of neglected shrubberies and broke up solid masses of rhododendrons by using more ferns, or flowers like the 'late blooming willow gentian', combined with plenty of lilies. She was not, however, one of those gardeners who decree the growing of a flower without any thought for whether it will survive the conditions on

Bergenias, mulleins and lilies were favourite Jekyll plants. Bergenia leaves have a tiresome habit of curling and browning, but these seen at Hestercombe have been kept meticulously clean.

offer. She knew exactly what was needed for the cultivation of every plant that she specified and, like Robinson, she gave amateur gardeners plenty of advice on how best to simulate a plant's natural environment.

Thoughtful and practical tips for amateurs made a change from the technical hints for professionals which the head gardeners had dispensed around the middle of the nineteenth century. Garden advice was now less a matter of manipulating the habits of plants than watching what they did. In the past, 'natural' effects were man-made. John Fleming, at Cliveden, had planted bluebells at the edges of woodland walks which was much admired and copied: Fleming, rather than nature, was credited with the example. Jekyll also popularized bluebells, but in a rather different way. 'A fine lesson and example is a wood of wild bluebells in May. It shows the value of doing one thing at a time and doing it largely and thoroughly well,' she wrote, foreshadowing the ecological approach of our own time. The colonies of self-seeding plants in the wild garden were in marked contrast to the display of cultivated exotics in a flower bed, or the bulbs planted out by the gross.

Where once the reaction had been an exclamation at the manpower needed to stage an effect, now everything had to look as though it happened naturally. In large gardens there were still plenty of gardeners to do the work, but this was not supposed to show. The Edwardians valued ease and comfort; while England was at peace a comfortable style of

gardening suited the prevailing mood. 'Art, like laughter, should be the language of happiness, and those who suffer should be silent,' wrote George Sitwell, who made a formal Italianate garden at Renishaw in Derbyshire. His garden lacked the variety of plants which Robinson and Jekyll wrote about, because he used sculpture rather than flowers to add that 'last touch of colour in a picture, which sets the whole canvas in a flame'. But it was nearer in mood to a Jekyll garden than to a Victorian one because it was a place to relax in and enjoy. Victorian gardens cannot have been very comfortable; as life loosened up, people as well as plants began to feel at home out of doors.

Grouping colours of one or two tones together was practised in Arts and Crafts borders. Sunset shades like these were placed far from mauves and pinks. The hottest colours often occupied the central section of the border, which would fade into blues at the far end to make it appear much longer.

195

CHAPTER 8

HEDGES, HERBS, HELLEBORES & GREENERY

'A kind of haphazard luxuriance which of course comes neither by hap nor hazard at all'

Cottages at Burghclere *by Stanley Spencer (1891–1959)*

THE FIRST HALF OF THE CENTURY WHICH SAW TWO WORLD WARS and the invention of the motor, finally brought everyone down to earth and back to the soil. But whether doing your own gardening became fashionable from necessity, or because of a general desire to spend more time out of doors is difficult to say. Between the wars, life in large country houses still went on almost as it had in its Victorian and Edwardian heyday. At Holker in Cumbria there were six enormous greenhouses kept going at full blast, with carnation houses and gardenia houses which survived the Great War, but the days of such places were numbered. Today there are comparatively few places run on this scale. The National Trust, which now owns the majority of Britain's great gardens, cannot afford to heat glass houses and fill walled gardens with produce for the house, and the handful of private gardeners who appear to keep things going in style would be found to be living in very reduced circumstances if their spending were compared with their budget earlier in the century. Economy had the effect of shrinking the scope of all gardens and making them more personal.

The gardens which lasted best, those which still influence the way we plan and plant today, all had owners who physically gardened. Some of them had gardeners too, but the day-to-day business of what was planted or pruned, or removed or encouraged was

Opposite: the Lutyens seat placed under the modern 'Constance Spry' rose at Mottisfont would not have been painted white in an Arts and Crafts garden, but would have been made in solid oak which silvers with age.

197

*Above: Gertrude Jekyll described delphiniums as
'the grandest blues of the flower year'. The large
hybrids, like these in the picture, were developed by
Blackman and Langdon early this century, but
Miss Jekyll preferred to grow her own plants from
seed, choosing 'Cantab' as the seed parent, finding
these better for her purposes than the named kinds,
of which she also had a fair collection.*

*Strong architectural layouts containing a profusion
of plants became the most admired style for gardens
in the twentieth century. At Buckland
Monachorum in Devonshire rare plants are
crammed cottage-fashion into enclosed spaces.*

Dead-heading the roses was a suitably lady-like occupation for a well-brought-up young girl between the Wars. Her attentions would have also been useful where pinks like 'Mrs Sinkins' were grown, as they are at Castle Howard in Yorkshire.

increasingly done not for money, but as a labour of love. Gertrude Jekyll popularized gardening as a hobby for the prosperous middle class and the new taste for fresh air and exercise may also have encouraged people to occupy themselves out of doors. Characters in Scott Fitzgerald's novels played tennis and sunbathed and their example was certainly followed by real people, but even the best game of tennis does not take all day. On the walk to the grass court the garden as a setting for the game and for social life, assumed a new importance. Indoors, flower arranging was fashionable and this also focused attention on the garden. In nineteenth-century establishments, where there was a gardener, it was his responsibility to organise the flowers indoors. But the twentieth-century lady of the house enjoyed 'doing the flowers' and took on this duty herself. For unmarried daughters in middle-class households between the wars, this was often the only occupation which gave them any status. Supervising the work of growing the flowers, deadheading the roses and planting out were all suitably ladylike occupations for a well-brought-up young girl. Like the Victorian Miss, who studied her botanical trophies with Linnaeus on her lap in the parlour, her modern descendant was in safe company with flowers.

'If only one could get hold of the children! ... catch them young and put them in a garden, with no other people of their own class forever teaching them by example what is ugly and unworthy and gross.' wrote Elizabeth von Arnim, the best-selling author of

Elizabeth and her German Garden, which was still popular throughout the twenties and thirties. Sentiments like these indicate that gardening was not only good for the complexion, it was also still a moral activity, although it was no longer quite in the puritan and spiritual tradition of the seventeenth-century orchard growers. The ethos now was nearer to that of the sound mind in the healthy body, but there was too an element of:

> *The kiss of the sun for pardon*
> *The song of the birds for mirth*
> *One is nearer God's Heart in a garden*
> *than anywhere else on earth.*
>
> (MRS GURNEY C 1910)

The gardens which lasted best after the economies imposed by two World Wars were those which had owners who bothered about the day-to-day business of growing plants. In the walled rose garden at Castle Howard the continuing interest of a distinguished modern gardener, James Russell, ensures the success of this comparatively new layout.

This tradition emerges in our own time where there is an underlying association of gardening with worthiness and endeavour. The use of the spade, contact with compost, raising seedlings, cherishing flowers, growing vegetables and pruning roses imply all sorts of virtuous qualities; hard work, thriftiness, gentleness, attention to detail, creativity and authority are all suggested. In reality, gardeners are not, of course, better people then anyone else when they go indoors. But the fact that they take plenty of exercise in the

Above: The former head gardener's house in the kitchen garden at Castle Howard looked out over rows of well-ordered vegetables. Today the garden empire is still ruled by the occupant of this house who has designed a modern garden to fill the view from his windows. The new breed of gardeners in the twentieth century take as much trouble as the old head gardeners, but their preoccupations are rather different.

The plantsman's garden at Docwra's Manor in Cambridgeshire shows the influence of Hidcote and Sissinghurst in its straight double borders closed by yew hedges.

The herb garden was developed into an ornamental feature after the 1920s. Herbs inspired much sentimentality and dipping into old herbals. The fennel seen here at Grimsthorpe Castle in Lincolnshire would have been encouraged in the gardens of flappers who cared about their figures. 'Both leaves, seeds and roots are much used in drink or broth to make people lean that are too fat,' wrote Culpeper, whose herbal was constantly quoted by ladies such as Eleanor Sinclair Rohde who made herbs popular.

The great green flowers of angelica also graced the newly planted herb gardens. This ornamental biennial is seen in a cottage garden near Bressingham in Norfolk.

In the 1920s many new rhododendrons and azaleas were sent home by plant collectors like Forrest and Kingdon Ward. At Killerton in Devon, which has a long tradition of growing plants from collected seed, the woodland garden glows with these Asiatic shrubs.

fresh air may make them easier to live with. Those who do their own gardening are, too, masters of their chosen world; few people are given such a chance to be dictators as gardeners. Professor Keith Thomas in his fascinating study of *Man and the Natural World* suggests that D.H. Lawrence had spotted the fact that gardens are a means of strengthening the owner's identity and adding to his self-esteem, when he wrote 'Most of this so-called love of flowers is merely this reaching out of possession and egoism: something I've got: something that embellishes *me*!' This is truer in the twentieth century than at any other time. E.F. Benson's novels also make fun of this tendency in the exchanges between Miss Mapp and Lucia, while one of Saki's best short stories highlights the discomfiture of Adela Pingsford when an ox gets into her garden. 'What kind of ox?' asks her neighbour:

'Oh I don't know what kind' snapped the lady. 'A common or garden ox to use the slang expression. It is the garden part that I object to. My garden has just been put straight for the winter and an ox roaming about in it won't improve matters. Besides there are the chrysanthemums just coming into flower.'

This social commentary on the owner-gardener by three different authors indicates how proprietorial people were becoming in the first half of this century. The gardens made by head gardeners had never really belonged to the people who owned them. The personal garden is a late development of modern times.

For whatever reason, it was just as well if everyone had begun to enjoy being out of doors with a garden tool in their hand. The conditioning which was started by Robinson and Jekyll and fanned by the cult of fresh air and property owning was very necessary when the Second World War started. Digging for victory replaced deadheading the roses; the tennis lawn was ploughed and put down to potatoes; and wives and daughters everywhere had to learn to use the spade, if they wanted to feed their families. The large gardens that were left untended by the gardeners who went to the war soon lost their definition. 'Look after the hedges, we can get the rest back later,' said the head gardener at Sissinghurst as he left to join the airforce. Only those, like Vita Sackville-West, who were prepared to do the work would bring their gardens through.

The first of the modern type of owner-gardeners was perhaps a quiet American called Lawrence Johnston, who started laying out Hidcote in Gloucestershire around 1907. He had had a cosmopolitan education which gave him a lifelong fondness for France and Italy, but England he loved best. He became a British citizen and settled in Northumberland

The garden at Knightshayes in Devonshire was made after the last War. It is the perfect woodland garden combining rare plants with native ones. Here, in the foreground, spurge and bluebells are underplanted among rhododendrons and azaleas.

Overleaf: Old-fashioned roses were used in preference to hybrid teas at Sissinghurst. Here a beautifully trained climber at Mottisfont repays hours of pruning and tying.

207

The brightly coloured late summer borders at Powis would also have appealed to the creator of Sissinghurst, who hankered after 'stuff which will give a lovely red colour in autumn'.

Page 209: As well as old roses, single roses were frequently chosen by discerning twentieth-century gardeners. The Gallica rose 'Complicata' seen here at Mottisfont was a favourite of Vita Sackville-West's. She considered it 'a real treasure, if you can give it room to toss itself about as it likes' and thought that 'its graceful untidiness is part of its charm'.

People connect Sissinghurst with the White Garden, but Vita Sackville-West loved colour. This startling clash of pinks, oranges, reds and purples at Powis Castle would probably have thrilled her.

where he farmed, until his mother gave him a small property in the Cotswolds at Hidcote Bartrim. Vita Sackville-West wrote about the place:

> When Major Johnston first acquired Hidcote in about 1907, he had nothing as a basis to his garden except one fine Cedar and two groups of Beeches. The rest was just fields, and I cannot believe that to any but a most imaginative eye it can have seemed a very promising site. There was no particular shape to it; standing high, it was somewhat wind-swept; there was nothing in the nature of old walls or hedges to afford protection; the soil was on the heavy side. It must have required immense energy, optimism, foresight, and courage to start transforming it into what it is today – a matured garden full of variety and beauty, the achievement of one man in his lifetime.

Lawrence Johnston's achievement was to create a series of interlocking plant kingdoms over which he ruled absolutely. His talents as a designer – he studied architecture before embarking on his garden – and his knowledge of plants were unusually accomplished. 'The combination of botanical knowledge and aesthetic taste is by no means axiomatic, but Major Johnston possessed it in the highest degree,' eulogized Vita Sackville-West. Hidcote's continuing appeal is in some part due to the out-of-this-world atmosphere which it sustains. It is not one secret garden but many set apart from the ordinary world. Italian Renaissance gardens probably suggested these enchanted spaces to the creator of Hidcote. Their private charm may hold a particularly enduring attraction for the Englishman whose home is his castle and whose garden is his kingdom, but their magic spellbinds everyone.

As well as mystery, Hidcote offers surprise and drama. A vista plunges between high green hedges, a dark ring of water fills the whole of one enclosure; a sacred tree dominates the great space of the Theatre lawn and a climb towards the sky unfolds in a view of Gloucestershire. Even if all the plants in the place were swept away, it would still be a beautiful garden. But the abundance of plants makes Hidcote doubly ensnaring. The luxuriance was what impressed Vita Sackville-West, 'a kind of haphazard luxuriance, which of course comes neither by hap nor hazard at all'. Here at last was a way of showing a vast collection of plants in a way that would not exhaust the visitor by its variety. Hidcote is a large garden, which needs several gardeners to maintain it, but it is not an overwhelming one. The lessons learnt from the management of its space provided an example that would be adopted by many owner-gardeners in the years to come.

Another American, Phyllis Reiss, who had been a neighbour of Johnston's in Gloucestershire, was responsible for a similar, but much smaller, garden at Tintinhull in Somerset which was started in 1933. Here a strong architectural layout also framed a series of outdoor 'rooms' designed to show off a variety of plants. As at Hidcote, the mood varied from room to room and everywhere there was an elegant balance between the restrained formality of the hedged enclosures and the rich abandon of the plants. The scale of the garden at Tintinhull is human and intimate; the careful choice of plants indicates the presence of a loving owner whose personality still breathes life into the garden. Not all of Phyllis Reiss's plants nor those of Lawrence Johnston survive in their gardens today, but the spirit of their plantings remain.

The Hon Victoria Sackville-West's well-known garden at Sissinghurst may have been inspired by Lawrence Johnston's work at Hidcote, which late in life she regarded as 'a flawless example of what a garden of this type should be'. Records of her meetings with

Opposite: Alliums and tulips line a straight and narrow path at Barnsley in Gloucestershire, where later laburnums will flower overhead.

Silver foliage and varying shades of green were all used to add depth and tone to the planting at Sissinghurst. Here, the fashion for silver plants has been adopted with so much enthusiasm that they have become a feature in their own right. This may not have been quite what Vita Sackville-West intended.

Johnston or of visits to Hidcote are scarce before 1941, when most of the work at Sissinghurst would have been completed. But the gardens have much in common, although the predominant atmosphere at Sissinghurst is more English and more ancient than the cosmopolitan and civilized feeling which prevails at Hidcote.

Where Johnston drew on the European Renaissance, Vita Sackville-West plundered her native past. Her private associations with her own forebears at Knole, the great Tudor mansion in Sevenoaks where she herself had grown up, and her love of the English countryside permeated her garden. She loved wild flowers and the species and old-fashioned roses which had gone out of favour when hybrid teas appeared. She was the opposite of Ruskin, who suggested that 'all dahlias, tulips, ranunculus and in general all florists' flowers should be avoided like the garlic', in that she relished old cottage plants and florists' flowers, like the auricula and the double primrose.

Herbs were also a feature of the garden and were, she wrote, 'encouragingly popular, with men as well as with the sentimentalists whom I know fatally in advance are going to say that it is full of old-world charm'. The herb garden, once it left the kitchen garden, and became ornamental around the 1920s, had this tendency to prompt nostalgic feelings. One of the earliest formal ornamental herb gardens at Broughton Castle in Oxfordshire actually spelled this out, with clipped santolina bushes announcing 'Ye herbe garden' at its entrance. Vita Sackville-West could be whimsical, but she deplored this kind of nostalgic sentimentality.

The plants at Sissinghurst were presented, as at Hidcote and Tintinhull, in a strong architectural layout. This was the responsibility of Harold Nicolson, who shared the creation of the garden with his wife. This partnership of talents, like the accomplishments of Lutyens and Jekyll, created a synthesis that was more than the sum of its parts. Although Vita Sackville-West was never at any stage a painter like Gertrude Jekyll, she treated her plants as an artist might have done. Her flair and flamboyant taste lit up every corner of the garden which, by all accounts, radiated her personality and style. To those for whom Sissinghurst suggests old roses and a white garden, the vibrancy of the planting in Vita Sackville-West's day might have come a surprise. As a young woman her clothes were said to have been startling and the room she enjoyed in her mother's house must have been dazzling:

> Her walls are of shiny emerald green paper, floor green; doors and furniture sapphire blue; ceiling apricot colour. Curtains blue and inside-curtains yellowish. The decoration of the furniture is mainly beads of all colours painted on the blue ground; even the door-plates are treated the same. I have 6 bright orange pots on her green marble mantelpiece, and there are salmon and tomato-colour cushions and lampshades. Pictures by Bakst, George Plank, Rodin, and framed in passe-partout ribbons.

The plants at Sissinghurst were often chosen to reflect their owner's dramatic taste and romantic temperament. 'Exaggeration, big groups; big masses,' were what Vita practised. 'My liking for gardens to be lavish is an inherent part of my philosophy' she wrote, causing her designer husband to complain of the tragedy of the romantic temperament, which sacrificed form to colour. 'She wants to put in "stuff which will give a lovely red colour in autumn". I wish to put in stuff which will furnish shape to the perspective.' Whatever the strains of making the garden, the end result has proved a cynosure for around half a century. Although Sissinghurst today contains far more plants than it did in Vita Sackville-West's day and is perhaps tidier than it was then (as well as much fuller of visitors), the place still shouts her name.

The Hidcote-Sissinghurst tradition remains a strong influence in our own time. The formula of disciplined geometry, the framed and luxuriant planting, suits small gardens of modern plantsmen with a sense of tradition and order. Like collections of tropical butterflies arranged in mahogany cases, the plants can be admired and studied both for their individual beauty and for their association with one another, as well as for the pattern they create together. Plant associations are a twentieth-century pre-occupation, Vita Sackville-West used to pick a flower of this and a leaf of that and hold them up against a background of other plants before she composed her pictures. Silver foliage and varying shades of green, different textures and shapes of leaves were all used to add tone and depth to the composition. This fine tuning of the relationship of one plant with another has become the hallmark of modern gardening.

In the years between the wars, there were, however, beginning to be other ways of disposing plants than in the style of Hidcote and Sissinghurst. Not everyone was inspired by the example set by the owner-gardeners with their succession of rooms outdoors. Dr Hampton, who practised as a psychiatrist, but who wrote about gardening under the name of Jason Hill, suggested in 1936 that 'the English garden, like the English dinner, is pretty much the same throughout the country. Most gardens consist of rose beds, herbaceous

border, lawn and rockery and in all but the very smallest there is a pergola garlanded with rambler roses' (these were generally Dorothy Perkins) which sounds as though things had hardly moved on since Queen Victoria's reign. The new breed of landscape architects, who had turned themselves into a professional association in 1929, took a more positive line than Jason Hill.

The most outspoken among them was a young designer called Christopher Tunnard, who later emigrated to America. He criticized quaint imitations of the Arts and Crafts style, which he felt were 'not of our time but of the sentimental past', in a powerful book, *Gardens in the Modern Landscape*, published in 1938. In it he suggested that if pleasure was admittedly found in machines and natural objects, or abstract paintings and tonal experiments, these were the influences that should shape the garden. He liked the idea of a Chilean pine taking on 'the precision of a machine in an architectural setting of a white walled courtyard'. Nature was no longer to be seen as a refuge, but as a stimulating environment. Indoors, the cult of functionalism made people see beauty in unlikely objects. The radiogram, for example, was given the place of honour in the drawing room because it fulfilled a purpose. Similarly, the design of the garden had to be seen to work. Christopher Tunnard's extreme precepts were, like all impassioned maxims, watered down. Gardeners who were not quite so committed to the dynamics of functionalism as

Silver leaves were also increasingly used to tone down colour in a border. At Mottisfont the woolly Stachys olympica *is associated with multicoloured aquilegias.*

Opposite: Curious plants like the prickly sea hollies, seen here at Denmans in Sussex, were first used to add form and texture to plantings in this century, when private gardeners began to choose plants for reasons other than their flowers. When the fleeting beauty of the cistus in the picture is over, the eryngiums will still provide something to look at.

217

At Shute House in Wiltshire, Sir Geoffrey Jellicoe created a mysterious garden of rich associations below the source of the river Nadder. Arches of wistaria cover the paths on either side of the water garden.

Tunnard produced some rather empty gardens, where the odd birch tree drooped in a lonely space.

Other landscape architects produced a milder version of the Modern Movement in commissioned work for private gardens, which resembled neither Hidcote nor Sissinghurst, nor Jason Hill's national prototype. Like Christopher Tunnard, they too saw the end of the sort of axial planning and monumental construction involved in the outdoor room style of garden. Along with George Bernard Shaw, the advocates of the Modern Movement believed that symmetry was the enemy of art, which brought them back to the thoughts of the eighteenth-century landscapers. 'The "landscape" style of the eighteenth century was our first great contribution to the art of garden design,' wrote Brenda Colvin, one of the founder members of the Landscape Institute, while her associate Sylvia Crowe, who did admire Hidcote, felt that it was 'natural that the tendency to abstract forms which has appeared in painting and the free shapes which have been accepted into the vocabulary of architecture should also find their way into garden design'. In the smaller gardens of the twentieth century, the eighteenth-century doctrine of the wavy line was scaled down to little more than a shrubbery and a curving path, by less capable hands than those of Colvin and Crowe. Their restraint and unity often eluded the amateur. (The ultimate reduction of the landscape garden is seen today in the modern island bed).

Geoffrey Jellicoe attempted something of his own which added another dimension to the Modern Movement. He remains the dominating figure in the history of twentieth-century landscape architecture, because he saw more than serpentine curves in landscape parks and felt that gardens should have a layer of meanings and associations below their superficial layout. Jellicoe's gardens were often intended to arouse feelings which may not have been experienced at the time of being in the garden, but which would drift to the surface of the mind, perhaps two or three days later. In an age when few cultural associations are shared this often failed, but the fact that there is an extra implicit layer in his designs gives them a quality and depth not often found in other gardens. Russell Page, who worked with Jellicoe was also influenced by the eighteenth century, in so far as he believed in consulting the genius of the place. He too thought deeply about the making of gardens and his book *The Education of a Gardener* (published in 1962) sums up his philosophy of design. Sadly he made very few gardens in England, but in spite of this he has emerged as one of the great designers of the twentieth century.

The planting which filled the Modern Movement's sinuous and abstract layouts was increasingly drawn from native material because native plants were felt to be more fitting than exotics or hybrids. They never jarred but provided harmony and serenity. In her book on *Garden Design*, the subtle qualities of species plants were praised by Sylvia Crowe and

The tapestry effect of the garden at Buckland Monachorum has something in common with the richly planted borders at Hidcote.

Overleaf: The soft grey plants at Northbourne Court in Kent give tone and depth to the colour scheme. Many of these were included in the White Garden at Sissinghurst. Another famous gardener, Margery Fish, also used many silver foliage plants and encouraged her readers to do the same.

Flat stone bridges lead the eye down the length of rill at Shute House in an orderly progression, but the planting is allowed to be exuberant.

Previous page: The acid green flowers of alchemilla and spurges were loved by Mrs Fish, who used them to set off brighter colours in much the same way as they are shown here at Powis Castle.

Opposite: A collector's garden at Abbotsbury in Dorset makes the most of the particularly mild climate.

wild trees were also recommended. 'Against the singing green of the early beech leaves, nothing can be more lovely than the white of the wild cherry.' Compare this with Nancy Mitford's description of the garden at Planes in *Love in a Cold Climate* (1945):

> You could hardly see any beautiful, pale, bright, yellow-green of spring, every tree appeared to be entirely covered with a waving mass of pink or mauve tissue-paper. The daffodils were so thick on the ground that they too obscured the green, they were new varieties of a terrifying size, either dead white or dark yellow, thick and fleshy; they did not look at all like the fragile friends of one's childhood.

This shows the sort of competition which the landscape architects and their followers faced.

Lack of form and contrast in the habit and foliage of plants was what made places like Planes so dull when the flowers were over, but gradually private gardeners began to appreciate these qualities and to choose plants for reasons other than their flowers. The cult of plantsmanship was not really developed in amateur gardens until after the Second

The Victorians liked gunnera for its exotic connotations, but twentieth-century gardeners used plants like this to add variety and change of scale to the landscape. Large leaves provide a rest for the eye in any planting. Hostas and bergenias can be used to similar effect in drier situations.

Previous page: The sculptured shapes of yew at Athelhampton in Dorset recall the enchanted spaces of Italian Renaissance gardens which had so much influence on Lawrence Johnston at Hidcote.

Opposite: Lily ponds were popular features in '30s gardens, along with pergolas supporting 'Dorothy Perkins' roses and herbaceous borders. At Athelhampton a beautifully designed pool makes a grand statement.

World War, which lies outside the scope of this book. However, the twentieth century saw a growing tradition of plant specialists who were lit up and excited by plants. E.A. Bowles did not need to find a plant growing in the wild to sing it a hymn of praise. His descriptions of the plants he cherished gave his readers the chance to see flowers as he did. 'I love this weird little flower', he wrote of *Hermodactylus tuberosus*, 'made up of the best imitation I have ever seen in vegetable tissues of dull green silk and black velvet – in fact it looks as if it had been plucked from the bonnet of some elderly lady of quiet tastes in headgear.' The objects of Mr Bowles's affectionate and observant tributes could be seen in his garden at Myddleton House, Enfield.

East Lambrook Manor in Somerset was another garden where a love of plants was displayed. Here Margery Fish grew flowers and shrubs with gusto. Her collection, that was started in 1937, was largely made during the war years when it contained many plants which were also present at Sissinghurst and Hidcote, but because it was smaller, the distractions were fewer. The plants were what mattered. It was perhaps the first of the plantsmen's gardens. Later in the fifties Margery Fish wrote about her garden and the plants that it contained and her advice described the new more subdued style of planting which was beginning to matter to thinking gardeners. Evergreens for all-year interest became important, so that the garden was enjoyable, even in winter. Architectural plants,

Page 228: Sir Geoffrey Jellicoe's formal spaces of water at Shute House suggest early English, as well as Mogul, gardens. The rich layers of meaning in his landscapes are designed to make the visitor think.

Page 229: At Trengwainton in Cornwall the stream is allowed to flow in a more natural style. Many garden designers in the middle of this century preferred the informality of nature to architectural gardens.

Harold Peto's long Italianate water garden at Buscot is unadorned with water lilies, which makes it a much more tranquil place than the pool at Athelhampton.

231

At Blenheim Achille Duchêne was engaged in the 1920s and '30s to make formal gardens below the house. These grand parterres illustrate the gathering interest in historical reconstructions.

Page 232: The mysterious pond at Abbotsbury provides a calm interlude in a garden of tropical vegetation.

Page 233: Arum lilies beside the water at Shute House make a change from tangled water lilies. They grow best in very damp places which are not too cold, so this southern garden suits them admirably.

which punctuated a flower bed and gave shape to a planting were vital and so were soft grey shrubs to add tone and depth to a colour scheme. Subtlety was the aim and Mrs Fish was particularly fond of green flowers. Hellebores, euphorbias, astrantias, acanthus, hebes, crane's bills, *Senecio greyi*, rue, phlomis and *Stachys olympica (S. lanata)* were some of the plants which evoked this new mood. This was to culminate in the work of Graham Stuart Thomas, whose books since the war years have done more to teach people about which plants to grow than any other source of advice.

Subtlety is not easy to sell and the imposition of universal taste has never been simple. In the twentieth century, that era of the 'Me' generation, perhaps Sylvia Crowe put it best when she acknowledged that:

> Today, because there is not the same solidarity of taste, and also because gardens are spread through a far larger section of society, there is a greater diversity of needs. For this reason, a modern garden style, showing the same uniform characteristics as previous traditions, is unlikely to emerge and should not be encouraged, for it would contradict one of the basis of

a true garden, in that it could not genuinely represent the character of its owner. Instead, the need of each owner should be developed into a garden individual to himself, and in the sincerity which such a garden expresses, it is likely also to give pleasure to others.

What gardens mean to their owners has differed in every century. The tensions between art and nature, privacy and prospect, or of public and personal life have altered the setting for the English house at every level of society almost as often as every two generations. What has been common to all gardens is that they express a current age's feelings about nature. They reveal, too, much about the aspirations of those who live in their time. Today when most gardens have become perhaps more superficial than at any other time, they say more about our materialism than our spirituality. For the time being at least, feelings do not furnish many gardens, but in this constantly shifting aspect of English life, change is never far away. A revival of interest in past values and a new sense of responsibility for the resources of the earth are already bringing another emphasis to the English garden. New impulses will give momentum to a different style and one which will tell generations to come as much about our time as we can learn of the past from the gardens which are gone.

The garden at Barnsley House is full of the sort of plants made popular by Margery Fish. Green euphorbias retain their freshness throughout the spring.

CHAPTER 9

POTTAGE, PEAS, PEACHES & PINEAPPLES

'I have always thought a kitchen garden a more pleasant sight than the finest orangerie or artificial greenhouse.'

Vegetable Garden at Charlton Park *by Thomas Robins.*

S
ELF-SUFFICIENCY IS A LUXURY TODAY, BECAUSE FEW PEOPLE CAN afford the time or the money to grow enough vegetables and fruit to feed themselves all the year round. It is much cheaper to pick a cabbage off the supermarket shelves, or a packet of peas from the freezer, than it is to supervise their growing out of doors. It was not always so. Until the twentieth century all gardeners set aside some space for growing their own food crops. In country districts, where communications were slow and fresh produce could only be bought once a week on market day, self-sufficiency was a necessity. There was no place for the amateur or the dilettante in the kitchen garden. If you could not grow what you ate, you starved.

Soup, or pottage, was the staple diet of the early English. Boiled cabbage with a few onions and plenty of parsley, and seasonal variations, appeared daily on the tables of nobles and peasants throughout the Middle Ages and continued to be the basic fare in poor households for hundreds of years. In medieval halls, where everyone ate together, those above the salt enjoyed more meat and fish than the lower orders, but the pottage was common to all. Cabbage, which was known as 'Colewort' or often simply 'Wort' had to be sown four times a year to provide a constant supply for this soup. 'Wurtys we must have both to master and to knave', wrote Mayster Jon Le Gardener who worked for the King at Windsor in the early fourteenth century, in a first practical gardening manual. This

Opposite: At Heale House in Wiltshire the traditional kitchen garden has a pool at its centre surrounded by fat domes of box. Tunnels of trained apple trees line the paths and flowers and vegetables are grown in a relaxed mixture.

Cucumbers were better known than marrows in Elizabethan England and a great deal of superstition was attached to their cultivation. 'Fair and big cucumbers' should be gathered 'at the full of the moon', suggested Thomas Hill. Today we rate size lower than flavour and these marrow plants in the kitchen garden at Ammerdown will be harvested while very young.

cabbage, which was a cut-and-come again variety, was much nearer to kale than to the modern full-headed varieties grown today. The pottage, which was boiled all day, occasionally had a few broad beans cooked in their pods, or some peas or leeks thrown in when they were in season, but the taste must have been predominantly flavoured cabbage water. Other herbs were added to ring the changes but they needed to be strong to be effective. Hyssop was popular and mustard seed was often used. Garlic, borage, marigolds, vinegar, beef dripping, nettles and docks were also reliable condiments for the pottage maker.

In small gardens the vital ingredients for flavouring pottage were grown alongside the herbs for household remedies and the flowers like honeysuckle and roses, which were beautiful and scented, as well as useful. The large gardens belonging to noblemen or to the Church had separate enclosed areas to feed the household, but although these were on a grander scale, the vegetables they contained were limited to the same varieties used by everyone. Kale, onions, parsley, garlic and leeks filled every kitchen garden. Where there was space, flax and hemp were grown to supply materials for home-made linen and sacking. But peas and beans were more often grown in fields than in kitchen gardens.

Henry VIII was guilty of the destruction of many monastery gardens, but his own enthusiasm for garden making did much to popularize new varieties of fruit and

vegetables. He had men scouring the Continent for apples, apricots, cherries and pomegranates, which were brought back for him to try in England. He sent his gardeners into the woods to dig up wild strawberries to plant in the garden and during his reign cucumbers and sallets (salads), as well as root vegetables such as carrots and parsnips, began to appear on tables all over England.

The Gardener's Labyrinth by Thomas Hill (or Didymus Mountain) summed up the horticultural knowledge acquired during the time of Henry VIII. The first edition of this growers' manual, aimed at Everyman and published in 1563, mentions lettuce, endive, chicory, artichokes, asparagus, beet, Blette (chard), turnips, carrots, radishes, parsnips, sorrel, spinach and fennel, which would all by this time have been familiar to ordinary people. The book was not entirely Thomas Hill's unaided work, but a compilation from existing herbals and Continental texts. It contained many intriguing tips and much advice that is still practical today. There are, for example, instructions for making early mole smokes out of nuts filled with brimstone or pitch; and hints on growing cucumbers which 'need much moisture in which they mightily joy'. Thomas Hill's description of an early kitchen garden, enclosed in hedges made of gooseberry, thorn, currants or sweetbriar, gives a good picture of the layout of an Elizabethan garden, but would not be out of place today.

> The owner or gardener ought to remember, that before he committeth seeds to the earth, the beds be disposed and troden out, into such a breadth and length, as best answereth to every plant and root, in that the beds to be sowen for the Navew [a brassica or a kind of rape] roots, ought to be troden out large and long; next to which may the beds for Coleworts and Cabbages be joyned of a sufficient breadth: to these next may you place beds of a reasonable breadth for the Rapes and Turen roots: then for a semely division in the Garden, may he tread out by those an Alley of three foot broad: next to which, if the Gardener will, may he dispose sundry beds together for divers kinds of hearbs, as the Arach, Spinedge, Rocket, Parcely, Sorrel, Beets, Speradge, Chervil, Borrage, Fenel, Dill, Mints, white Poppy , and sundry others. Next joyning to these, may the owner or Gardener place an other Alley of three foot broad, by which, frame beds for the Leeks and Cives: and to the next, may the Gardner joyne beds for the Onions and Chibouls; by these next, the Scalions and Garlick in two beds disposed. Then level out by these, an Alley of three foot and a half broad, to which the Gardener my adjoyne many beds about for borders, serving as well for the keeping in of the savours, as for hedges, and pot-hearbs for the Winter.

This type of arrangement of beds (rather like those in modern allotments) could still occasionally be seen in the second half of the eighteenth century. An anonymous panoramic view of Ashcombe in Wiltshire, painted around 1770, shows a series of strip beds for vegetables and flowers within a rough triangle of wall. In less provincial gardens, however, the layout of the beds after the end of the seventeenth century was generally in a four-square plan, as it had been in Renaissance gardens. Small gardens (that is those of an

Runner beans from the New World were often grown for ornament as much as for eating, and were used to shade arbours in kitchen gardens. Their decorative value today is underestimated.

The kitchen garden at Grimsthorpe Castle in Lincolnshire is still laid out on the old four square principle, with vegetables grown in meticulously straight rows. In pre-twentieth-century gardens boys were paid to shoo the birds away. Netting is more practical but less humane.

At Oare House in Wiltshire espaliered apples have turned knobbly with age. This efficient technique still produces huge amounts of fruit in a restricted space.

acre or less) would be quartered, but larger ones would be subdivided into eigths or sixteenths. At the main intersections there were often wells or tanks for watering and, as well as the central paths, there were paths and beds following the line of the enclosure. These outer borders were kept for fruit and salad crops, or for plants which needed permanent places.

The four-square plan, with subdivisions for different types of vegetables, continued to prevail as a layout through all the changes to the garden outside the kitchen enclosure. Formal gardens came and went, the landscape movement swept away all man-made barriers, but in the kitchen garden a constant useful order, with a few changes to the crops, continued in much the same spirit for hundreds of years. Enclosures (which kept rabbits out and provided shelter for early vegetables and fruit) were always an important feature and, by the end of the seventeenth century, most kitchen gardens of any size were surrounded by walls, rather than by hedges, or wattle hurdles. There was an added reason for screening the kitchen garden in the eighteenth century. Its formal rows of vegetables and utilitarian atmosphere were not in keeping with the natural flowing lines of park and views. Kitchen gardens were sited a long way from the house in landscape gardens. They had a very old-fashioned look with their borders of flowers, rolled walks and neatly trained trees. Even the nails for fastening the fruit to the walls were set out in formal patterns. The

whole enclosure was a refuge for the symmetry which had been abolished outside its walls. It could be admired from a central arbour or seat set at the top of the central path, under the south-facing wall and flanked by fan-trained fruit. Occasionally the head gardener's house was built within the kitchen garden, and this too became an element in the formal design. It was also very convenient for supervising the unending work that went into the running of this empire.

Kitchen gardens may have been banished from the larger garden but they were still enjoyed and visited, even by the intellectuals who hastened the demise of the formal garden. Addison was not ashamed to write, 'I have always thought a kitchen garden a more pleasant sight than the finest orangerie or artificial Greenhouse.' He liked to survey his rows of colworts and cabbages, with 'a thousand nameless pot herbs springing up in their full fragrancy and verdure'. Some writers even indicated that they were not unfamiliar with growing their own vegetables. A little known mid eighteenth-century poet, Henry Jones, composed eight verses 'on a Fine crop of peas being spoiled by a Storm', which describes the effect of 'one tempestuous hour' on 'the labours of a year'. The large landowners were not as emotional in their response to growing vegetables as these literary men, but their interest in crop rotation and good husbandry extended to the kitchen garden, where cultivation reached a high point around the end of the eighteenth century.

Forcing pots for rhubarb and seakale seen here at West Green House in Hampshire provide early and tender fruit and vegetables. Seakale was a favourite late-eighteenth-century delicacy.

In the eighteenth century the kitchen garden was a refuge for the symmetry which had been abolished outside its walls. Straight paths edged with box hedges can be seen through a circular opening at West Green House.

Fruit growing in particular was raised to a fine art. In the eighteenth century there were heated walls with built-in fireplaces which directed the heat up the slanting flues lining the brickwork. Later a similar arrangement pumped hot water through pipes fed by a boiler to protect or ripen tender fruit. Gardeners stoked the fires all through the night and rose at dawn to check the state of their crops. At the first sign of frost, or too much rain, mats or screens were hauled into position. When the weather behaved, but the birds threatened, nets had to be rolled down from hooks on the wall to keep their greed at bay. Hours of toil and cartloads of fuel and dung lay behind each perfect peach, apricot or grape that reached the table.

Centrally heated walls were not enough for fruit which required tropical conditions, like pineapples. These needed extravagant heating and much larger areas of glass than the conventional orangery, which generally had a covered roof and relied on little more than pits of steaming manure to raise the temperature. By the end of the eighteenth century, even Yorkshire was a hot-bed of pineapples, and squires competed with one another to grow and sell the most. Home-grown paw-paws, melons and bananas were also achieved. Fruit has never been so lavishly or beautifully grown as it was in the eighteenth and nineteenth century.

Vegetables were equally stage-managed. There was asparagus at Christmas, and peas and lettuces while snow lay on the ground. All these were planted in hot-beds, which were filled with dung and covered at night with bell jars. If there was room to bring them indoors they were forced in pots in the glass house, but most vegetables were generally grown out of doors in the sort of conditions provided by a modern heated frame.

Flowers for cutting were an important feature in kitchen gardens. Louis XIV's gardener, who arranged the flowers at Versailles, probably brought the tradition of growing them for picking to England. During the reign of William and Mary there was a regular order for cut flowers for the royal rooms at Whitehall, which was supplied by George London. As flowers disappeared from the garden proper, they were increasingly found in borders in the kitchen garden. In the eighteenth century kitchen gardens were delightfully flowery and often had borders lining the central path full of old-fashioned flowers, which were grown as much for their decorative value out of doors, as they were to fill vases inside. The borders were generally backed with espalier apples, or a light fence of gooseberries and at the edge a low box hedge, which harboured hundreds of snails, marked the division of path and bed.

In the Victorian age gardeners were too busy in their hot-houses to bother with perennials. Paxton had decreed that 'all such plants as are perfectly hardy' had no longer any place in the garden. As a result kitchen gardens often became nothing more than backrooms for the display garden. Loudon remarked that no member of the royal family would ever think of walking into the kitchen garden at the beginning of the nineteenth century and the new emphasis on horticultural technique may have made these once beautiful and productive places less attractive to visit for everyone. However, Queen Victoria did enjoy her newly refurbished kitchen garden which covered thirteen acres at Frogmore. Here the cabbages were 'all dressed in line, like soldiers on parade' for her reviewing. An account in the *Gardeners' Chronicle* of 1849 described the four main compartments that were designed to look their best from the gardener's house, where there were two rooms kept for Queen Victoria and Prince Albert. But the 'admirable order and the precision with which everything is placed so as to gratify the eye by the display of the most exact symmetry' contained no flowers.

The head gardeners' domains were very different from the old-fashioned kitchen gardens which George Eliot and Disraeli described so lovingly in their novels. The places where vegetables and flowers were combined in 'half-neglected abundance' were rare enough to warrant purple passages of prose. When the Arts and Crafts gardeners, like William Robinson and Gertrude Jekyll, looked for inspiration they found it in cottage

Opposite: Box hedges are notorious harbourers of snails, but they form an unbeatable frame for traditional vegetables at Heale House.

Flowers have been grown in kitchen gardens for hundreds of years. In the seventeenth century London grew them in cutting borders for the house. In the eighteenth century old-fashioned plants which were no longer welcome in the garden proper lined the central paths. At Batemans the tradition is kept up with early varieties such as Solomon's Seal and other shade-loving plants grown under trained fruit trees.

gardens or kitchen gardens, where the traditional muddle of vegetables and flowers prevailed. 'Much as I love the flower garden and the woodland, I am by no means indifferent to the interest and charm of the kitchen garden,' wrote Gertrude Jekyll, who 'often strolled for pure pleasure among the vegetables'. But in her kitchen gardens the hardy flower borders were restored (sometimes with grass paths which are less than practical where vegetables are grown).

The massive labour forces needed to manage the walled gardens of England dwindled after the First World War. It became increasingly hard to find the immaculate engine room of the Victorian kitchen garden or the untidy charm of the lesser old-fashioned family gardens. During the Second World War, digging for victory produced enough food to feed armies of evacuees, but there was no heat for tender crops and little time for fruit. Kitchen gardens during the war years produced more pottage than pineapples. After the war very few walled gardens continued to be kept up. Market gardens, riding schools, Christmas trees, tennis courts or swimming pools were all tried as a method of filling the space where once dozens of gardeners had grown orderly rows of food for the house. More often still, weeds occupied what used to furnish a head gardener's pride. Today there are a few kitchen gardens in good order, but anyone who organizes the work of growing fruit and vegetables will admit that it takes more time than most other garden operations. It is an

indication of this drain on resources that the National Trust runs to only a few semi-cultivated kitchen gardens. Nothing approaching the intensive cultivation of earlier examples has been attempted. The loss of the full-blown kitchen garden is one of the tragedies in the history of gardening.

There has been a renewal of interest in the kitchen garden in the twentieth century. The cult of the potager has revived old ways of growing vegetables for ornament as well as for the table. At Grimsthorpe arches of runner beans add interest to the traditional layout.

GARDENS FEATURED IN THE BOOK

AMMERDOWN
Radstock
Bath BA3 5SH
Open: Spring and Summer Bank Hols only

ARLEY HALL
nr Northwich
Cheshire
Tel: 056 585 353
Open: End March–Oct, Tues–Sun and Bank Hol. Mondays 2–6

ATHELHAMPTON
nr Puddletown
Dorset
Tel: 03058 48363
Open: Easter–Oct, 2–6 Wed, Thurs, Sun, Good Friday and Bank Hols

BARNSLEY HOUSE GARDEN
Barnsley, nr Cirencester
Gloucestershire
Tel: 028 574 281
Open: All year round, Mon–Sat 10–6

BATEMAN'S
Burwash, East Sussex
Tel: 0435 882302
Open: End March–end Oct, Sun–Wed and Good Friday 11–6

BELSAY HALL
Belsay
Newcastle on Tyne
Tel: 066 181 636
Open: Good Friday–Sept 30 10–6; Oct–Maundy Thursday 10–4

BLENHEIM PALACE
Woodstock
Oxford OX7 1PX
Tel: 0993 811325
Open: Mid March–Oct 31, daily 10.30–5.30

BOWOOD HOUSE AND GARDEN
Calne, Wilts
Tel: 0249 812102
Open: End March–Mid Oct, daily 11–6

BUCKLAND MONACHORUM
Yelverton
Devon
Tel: 082 285 4769
Open: April-Sept, daily noon–5

CAMELLIA GREENHOUSE
Chiswick House, Burlington Lane
London W4
Tel: 01–994 5669
Open: Feb–Oct, daily 10–5

CASTLE HOWARD
York
North Yorkshire
Tel: 065 384 333
Open: March 20–end Oct, daily 10–4.30

CHATSWORTH
Bakewell
Derbyshire
Tel: 024 688 2204
Open: End March–end Oct, daily 11.30–4.30

CHICHELEY HALL
Newport Pagnell
Buckinghamshire
Tel: 023 065 252
Open: End March–May 30, Aug 6–Sept 24, Suns and Bank Hol. Mons. 2.30–6

CHRISTCHURCH COLLEGE
Oxford
St Aldgates (Meadow Gate)
Open: Daily 7–dusk

CHURCH OF ST. MARY OF LAMBETH
The Tradescant Trust
Lambeth Palace Road
London SE1 7JU
Tel: 01–373 4030
Open: Weekdays 11–3, Sundays 10.30–5, Closed Saturdays

CLAREMONT LANDSCAPE GARDEN
Esher
Surrey
Open: All year round daily 9–7

CLIVEDEN
Maidenhead
Buckinghamshire
Tel: 06286 5069
Open: March–Dec, daily 11–6

COTEHELE HOUSE
Cadstock
Cornwall
Tel: 0579 50434
Open: Daily, sunrise to sunset

CRANBOURNE MANOR GARDENS
Cranbourne
Dorset
Tel: 072 54 248
Open: April–Sept, Weds 9–5
Garden Centre: Tues–Sats 9–5, Suns 2–5. Closed Jan. and Feb.

DENMANS
Fontwell
nr Chichester
East Sussex
Tel: 024 354 2808
Open: Mar 21–Oct 29, daily 10–5. Closed Mondays except Bank Hols.

DOWCRA'S MANOR
Shepreth
Royston
Cambridgeshire
Tel: 0763 60235/61473
Open: Various days during the year: telephone for times and dates

FARINGDON HOUSE
Oxfordshire
Not open to the public

FARNBOROUGH HALL
nr Banbury
Oxfordshire
Tel: 029 589 593
Open: April–end Sept, Weds, Sats and May Day Bank Hol. 2–6.
Grounds and Terrace Walks Thurs and Fri (not Good Friday) 2–6

FLINTHAM HALL
nr Newark
Nottinghamshire
Tel: 0636 525214
Open: Last Sunday in June each year

GLENDURGAN
Helford River
Cornwall
Tel: 0208 74281
*Open: Mar–end Oct, Mon, Wed and Fri
10.30–5.30*

GREAT DIXTER
Northiam
East Sussex
Tel: 079 74 3160
*Open: Good Fri–Sun Oct 15, daily (closed Mon
except Bank Hols) and weekends of Oct 21–22
and 28–29 (2–5) and May 27–29 (11–5)*

GRIMSTHORPE CASTLE
Bourne
Lincolnshire
Tel: 077 832 278
*Open: July 30–Sept 3 daily (closed Mon and Fri
but open Aug 28) 2–6*

HASELEY COURT
Little Haseley
Oxfordshire
Tel: 0844 279 500
*Open to the public 2 or 3 days per year for
charity. Telephone for dates and times.*

HATFIELD HOUSE
Hatfield
Hertfordshire
Tel: 070 72 62823/72738
*Open: March 25–2nd Sunday Oct. West Gdn,
daily 11–6; East Gdn, Mondays 2–5*

HEALE GARDENS AND PLANT CENTRE
Woodford, nr Salisbury
Wiltshire
Tel: 072 273 504
Open: All year round, 10–5

HELMINGHAM HALL
Ipswich
Suffolk
Tel: 047 339 363
Open: April 30–Oct 1, Sundays only 2–6

HESTERCOMBE HOUSE AND GARDENS
Cheddon Fitzpaine
Taunton
Somerset
Tel: 0823 87 2222
*Open: All year round, Mon–Fri 9–5; Sat and
Sun 2–5*

THE HIGH BEECHES
Handcross
West Sussex
Tel: 0444 400 589
*Open: Easter Mon–17 June and 18 Sep–29 Oct
1–5, daily except Weds and Suns, Spring Bank
Hols 10–5, 6 Aug 11–6 Traditional
Haymaking 29 Oct Special Event 10–5*

IFORD MANOR
Bradford on Avon
Wiltshire
Tel: 022 16 3146
*Open: May–Aug, daily and Summer Bank Hols
2–5*

KILLERTON
nr Exeter
Devonshire
Tel: 0392 881345
Open: All year round, daily 11–dusk

KINGSTON LACY
nr Wimborne Minster
Dorset
Tel: 0202 883402
Open: Mar 25–Oct 29, Sat–Wed 12–6

KNIGHTSHAYES COURT
nr Tiverton
Devonshire
Tel: 0884 254665
Open: 1 April–31 Oct, daily 11–6

LEORNARDSLEE GARDENS
nr Horsham
West Sussex
*Open: April 15–June 18, daily 10–6; July, Aug,
Sept, weekends only 12–6; Oct weekends,
10–5*

LEVENS HALL
nr Kendal
Cumbria
Tel: 053 95 60321
Open: Easter Sun–end Sept, Sun–Thurs 10–5

LITTLE MORETON HALL
Congleton
Cheshire
Tel: 0260 272018
*Open: March and Oct, Sat and Sun 1.30–5.30;
April–end Sept 11.30–5.30 daily except Tues
incl. Bank Hols.*

LYME PARK
Disley
Cheshire
Tel: 0663 62023
*Open: Mar 24–Sept 30, daily 11–6; Oct 1–April
1, daily 11–4*

MELBOURNE HALL
Melbourne
Derbyshire
Tel: 033 16 2502
*Open: April–Sept, Wed, Sat, Sun and Bank Hols
2–6*

MOTTISFONT ABBEY
Mottisfont
Hampshire
Tel: 0794 40210
*Open: April–end Sept, daily dawn–dusk; Rose
Garden, Tues–Sun 7–9 during the season*

NEWBY HALL
Ripon
North Yorkshire
Tel: 0423 322 583
*Open: Mar 24–Oct 29, daily 11–5; closed Mons
except Bank Hols.*

NEW COLLEGE
Oxford
Oxfordshire
Tel: 0865 52275
Open: Term, daily 2–5; Vacs, daily 11–5

NORTHBOURNE COURT
Deal
Kent
Tel: 0304 360 813
*Open: Various Sundays throughout the summer,
telephone for dates and times*

OARE HOUSE
Not open to the public

PAINSHILL PARK
Portsmouth Road, Cobham
Surrey
Tel: 0932 68113
Open: April 15–Oct 14, Sats 1–6

PENJERRICK HOUSE
Mawnan Smith, nr Falmouth
Cornwall
Open: Mar–Sept, Weds and Suns 1.30–4.30

POWIS CASTLE
Welshpool
Gwynned
Tel: 0938 4336
*Open: June, Sept–5 Nov, Weds–Suns 12–5;
July & Aug, Tue–Sun 11–6*

RIEVAULX ABBEY
nr Helmsley
North Yorkshire
Tel: 04396 228
*Open: Good Friday–Sept 30, daily 10–6; Oct
1–Maundy Thurs daily 10–4; closed Mons.*

ROUSHAM HOUSE
Steeple Ashton
Oxfordshire
Tel: 0869 47110
Open: All year round, daily 10–4.30

ST PAULS WALDEN BURY
Whitwell, nr Hitchin
Hertfordshire
Tel: 043 887 229/218
Open: occasionally for charity, telephone for dates and times.

SEZINCOTE
Moreton in Marsh
Gloucestershire
Open: All year round, Thurs, Fri and Bank Hol. Mons 2–6

SHERINGHAM PARK
Upper Sheringham
Norfolk
Tel: 0263 733 084
Open: All year round, daily dawn–dusk

SHRUBLANDS HALL
Coddenham
nr Stowmarket
Suffolk
Tel: 0473 830 221
Open occasionally to the public by arrangement with the Red Cross. Telephone for details

SHUTE HOUSE
nr Shaftesbury
Dorset SP7 9DG
Open once or twice a year for charity.

SISSINGHURST CASTLE
Sissinghurst
Kent
Tel: 0580 712 850
Open: Mar 24–Oct 15, Tue–Fri 1–6.30, Sat, Sun and Good Fri 10–6.30, closed all Mondays

SOMERLEYTON HALL
nr Lowestoft
Suffolk
Open: Easter Sun–June 1, Thurs, Suns and Bank Hols 2–5.30; June 1–Oct 1, Sun–Thurs 2–5.30

STOURHEAD
Stourton, nr Mere
Wiltshire
Tel: 0747 840 348
Open: All year round, daily 8–7 (or dusk if later)

STOWE COLLEGE
Buckingham
Buckinghamshire
Open: Mar 24–April 16, July 9–Aug 28, daily 12–dusk

STUDLEY ROYAL
Sawley Rippon
Yorks
Tel: 076 586 333
Open: All year round, daily 10–sunset

TRENGWAINTON
Penzance Cornwall
Tel: 0736 63021
Open: Mar 1–Oct 1, Wed–Sat 11–6; Bank Hol Mons 11–6; Mar and Oct daily 11–5

TUDOR GARDEN
Southampton University
Southampton
Hampshire
Tel: 0703 23855
Open: All year round, Tues–Sat 10–1 and 2–5; Sun 2–5; closed Mondays

WALLINGTON HOUSE
Cambo
Northumberland
Tel: 067 074 283
Open: Walled Garden, Easter–end Sept, 10–7 (or dusk if earlier); Oct, 10–6; Nov–Easter, 10–4. Grounds, all year round, dawn–dusk

WESTBURY COURT GARDEN
Westbury on Severn
Gloucestershire
Tel: 045 276 461
Open: Mar 25–end Oct, Weds–Suns, 11–6; Bank Hols 11–6

WEST GREEN HOUSE
nr Witney
Hampshire
Open: Mar 26–end Sept, Wed, Thur and Suns 2–6

WEST WYCOMBE PARK
West Wycombe
Buckinghamshire
Tel: 0494 24411
Open: April and May, Mon–Thurs 2–6; Easter, May Day and Spring Bank Hols, Sun & Mon 2–6; closed Good Friday; June–Aug, Sun–Thurs 2–6

BIBLIOGRAPHY

This book could not have been written without the inspiration and scholarship of others. The following list of books consulted is not exhaustive, but it includes my major sources. All those mentioned would provide additional reading for anyone interested in pursuing the subject further.

BACKGROUND

G. M. Trevelyan *English Social History*
Keith Thomas *Man and The Natural World*
Mark Girouard *Life in the English Country House*
Edmund Burke *Enquiries into the Origin of our Ideas of the Sublime and Beautiful*
Archibald Alison *On Taste*
William Morris *Hopes and Fears for Art*
Kenneth Clark *Landscape into Art*
Nicholas Pevsner *The Englishness of English Art*
David Cecil *Visionary and Dreamer*
David Watkins *The English Vision*
V & A *Rococo* Exhibition 1984
Tate Gallery *Landscape in Britain* Exhibition 1973
Jonathan Wordsworth *William Wordsworth and the Age of English Romanticism* Exhibition 1987
John Harris *The Artist and the Country House*
Andrew Clayton-Payne *Victorian Flower Gardens*
Penelope Hobhouse and Christopher Wood *Painted Gardens*
N.A.C.F. *Prospects of Town and Park* (loan exhibition Colnaghi 1988)

GENERAL GARDEN HISTORY

Ray Desmond *Bibliography of British Gardens*
Miles Hadfield *A History of British Gardening*
Derek Clifford *A History of Garden Design*
Christopher Thacker *The History of Gardens*
Fleming and Gore *The English Garden*
Jellicoe, Goode and Lancaster *The Oxford Companion to Gardens*
John Harris *The Garden* (V & A Exhibition)
John Harris *The Glory of the Garden* (Sothebys Exhibition)
Graham Stuart Thomas *Gardens of the National Trust*
Edward Hyams *English Cottage Gardens*
Anne Scott-James *The Cottage Garden*
David Stuart *The Kitchen Garden*
Alice M. Coats *Flowers and their Histories*
John Fisher *The Origins of Garden Plants*

ANTHOLOGIES

Dixon, Hunt and Willis *The Genius of the Place*
Best and Boisset *Leaves from the Garden*
David Waters *The Garden in Victorian Literature*
Ursula Buchan *An Anthology of Garden Writing*
Anne Scott-James *The Language of the Garden*

JOURNALS GARDEN HISTORY

The Journal of Garden History
Surveys and Management Plans of the National Trust

CHAPTERS 1 AND 2

John Harvey *Mediaeval Gardens*
Teresa McLean *Medieval English Gardens*
Coulton *Life in the Middle Ages*
John Harvey *Early Gardening Catalogues*
Roy Strong *The Renaissance Garden in England*
Thomas Hill *The Gardener's Labyrinth*
William Lawson *A New Orchard and Garden*
Francis Bacon *Of Gardens*
Christopher Morris (ed.) *Illustrated Journeys of Celia Fiennes*
Thomas Hanmer *The Garden Book of Sir Thomas Hanmer*
Kenneth Woodbridge *Princely Gardens: The Origins and Development of the formal French style*
Prudence Leith-Ross *The John Tradescants*
John Prest *The Garden of Eden*
Jacques and van der Horst *The Gardens of William and Mary*
Journal of Garden History *Anglo Dutch Garden in the age of William and Mary*
David Green *Gardener to Queen Anne*
John Evelyn *Diary*

CHAPTERS 3 AND 4

Peter Willis *Charles Bridgeman and the English Landscape Garden*
David Jacques *Georgian Gardens*
John Dixon Hunt *Garden and Grove*
John Dixon Hunt *The Figure in the Landscape*
Kenneth Woodbridge *Landscape and Antiquity*
E. Malins *English Landscape and Literature*
William Chambers *Dissertation on Oriental Gardening*
Horace Walpole *Essay on Modern Gardening*
Maynard Mack *Alexander Pope a Life*
Margaret Jourdain *The Work of William Kent*
Dorothy Stroud *Capability Brown*
Christopher Hussey *The Picturesque*
William Gilpin *On Pictures and Beauty*
Arthur Young *Tours of England*
James Thomson *The Seasons*
Thomas Hogg *A Treatise on the Carnation*
Mark Laird *Planting Plans for Eighteenth Century Wildernesses* (York University)
John Harvey *The Availability of Hardy Plants in the late Eighteenth Century*
James Meader *Planter's Guide or Pleasure Gardener's Companion*

CHAPTERS 5 AND 6

William Cobbett *Rural Rides*
Dorothy Stroud *Humphry Repton*
Carter, Goode and Laurie *Humphry Repton* V & A Exhibition
Humphry Repton *Observations on the Theory and Practice of Landscape Gardening*

BIBLIOGRAPHY — ACKNOWLEDGEMENTS

Pückler Muskau *Pückler's Progress* (trans. Flora Brennan)
J. C. Loudon *In Search of English Gardens*
J. C. Loudon *The Suburban Gardener and Villa Companion*
Jane Loudon *Practical Instructions in Gardening for Ladies*
David Elliston Allen *The Victorian Fern Craze*
Brent Elliott *Victorian Gardens*
David Stuart *The Garden Triumphant*
Canon Ellacombe *In a Gloucestershire Garden*
Dean Hole *A Book about the Garden*

CHAPTERS 7 AND 8
Audrey Le Lievre *Miss Willmott of Warley Place*
William Robinson *The English Flower Garden*
William Robinson *The Wild Garden*
Gertrude Jekyll *A Gardener's Testament*
Gertrude Jekyll *Wood and Garden*
Jekyll and Hussey *Garden ornament*
Penelope Hobhouse *Gertrude Jekyll on Gardening*
Jane Brown *Gardens of a Golden Afternoon*
Reginald Blomfield *The Formal Garden in England*
Inigo Triggs *Formal Garden in England and Scotland*
Avray Tipping *Gardens Old and New* (Country Life)

E. A. Bowles *My Garden in Spring . . . in Summer*
Victoria Glendinning *Vita*
V. Sackville-West *In your Garden*
V. Sackville-West *In your Garden Again*
V. Sackville-West *More for your Garden*
V. Sackville-West *Even more for your Garden*
Anne Scott-James *Sissinghurst*
Jane Brown *The English Garden in our Time*
Sylvia Crowe *Garden Design*
F. Clark *The Sense of Beauty in the Eighteenth, Nineteenth and Twentieth Century*
Christopher Tunnard *Gardens in the Modern Landscape*
Peter Shepherd *Modern Gardens*
Geoffrey Jellicoe *Guelph Lectures on Landscape Design*
Russell Page *The Education of a Gardener*
Margery Fish *A Flower for Every Day*

CHAPTER 9
David Stuart *The Kitchen Garden*
Thomas Hill *The Gardener's Labyrinth*
G. Jacob *The Country Gentleman's Vade Mecum*
William Lawson *A New Orchard and Garden*

ACKNOWLEDGEMENTS

THE PUBLISHERS ARE VERY GRATEFUL TO THE NATIONAL TRUST FOR PERMISSION to photograph several of their gardens, also to his Grace the Duke of Marlborough for permission to photograph the gardens of Blenheim Palace, to the Royal Horticultural Society for permission to photograph the gardens at Wisley, and to the owners of Heale House, Warwick Castle and all the other privately owned gardens in the book for permission to photograph them.

BOTANICAL ILLUSTRATIONS
William Curtis (1746—99): *Lilac* 127; E.T. Archive.

George Ehret (1708—70): *Deep Purple Lilac* 67; *Carnations* 86; *Magnolia* 87; *'Rosa Mundi'* 98; *Peony* 108; Victoria & Albert Museum (Bridgeman Art Library).

W.H. Finch after Sir Joseph Hooker (1817—1911): *Rhododendron* 161; Royal Botanic Gardens, Kew (Bridgeman Art Library).

Jenny Jowett: *Himalayan Blue Poppy* 212; *Hellebores* 215; *Rose hips* 235.

W.J. Linton (1812—98): *Sweet William* 155; Victoria & Albert Museum (Bridgeman Art Library).

Alexander Marshall: *Anemones* 57; British Museum

Jacques Le Moyne de Morgues (1530—88): *Wild Violets* 14; *Red Clover* 22; *Pink Rose* 29; *Marigolds* 31; Victoria & Albert Museum (Bridgeman Art Library).

Marianne North (1830—90): *Geranium* 122; *Roses* 133; Victoria & Albert Museum (Bridgeman Art Library).

Lillian Snelling (1879—1972): *Primula* (Forbesii) 169; *Campanula* (garganica Miss Payne) 195; Lindley Library (Bridgeman Art Library).

Emanuel Sweert: *Irises* from 'Theatrum Florae' (1612) 57; Royal Botanic Gardens, Kew (Bridgeman Art Library).

Miss Williamson (1905): *Iris* (Monspur) 182; Lindley Library (Bridgeman Art Library).

Dr Woodville (1790): *Myrtle* 95; L'Acquaforte, London (Bridgeman Art Library).

Artichoke 239; Victoria & Albert Museum (Bridgeman Art Library).

From 'Album Bennary': *Tomatoes* 247; Royal Botanic Gardens, Kew (E.T. Archive).

From 'The Collection of Flowers drawn from Nature': *Tulips* 50; Lindley Library (Bridgeman Art Library).

From 'Flora Luxuriana' (1789—91): *Polyanthus* 109; Royal Botanic Gardens, Kew (Bridgeman Art Library).

The paintings are reproduced by gracious permission of the following: 8 Chatsworth Settlement Trustees; 11 H.M. The Queen; 33 Yale Centre for British Art, New Haven; 59 Christie's, London (Bridgeman Art Library); 89 Private Collection (Sotheby & Co. photo); 111 Bristol City Museum and Art Gallery (Bridgeman Art Library); 114 British Library (Bridgeman Art Library); 135 British Library; 163 Christopher Wood Gallery, London (Bridgeman Art Library); 197 Fitzwilliam Museum, Cambridge; 237 Cheltenham Museum & Art Gallery (Bridgeman Art Library).

INDEX

Abbotsbury 223, 234
Addison 67, 78, 86, 243
Aislabie, John 61, 64, 75, 78, 79
Albert, Prince 127, 244
Albury 57
Allingham, Helen 155, 161, 164
Alnwick 98
Ammerdown 178, 238
Anne of Denmark 30
Arcadia 50, 53, 54, 71, 83
Archer, Thomas 64
Argyll, Duke of 102
Aristeppus 82
Arley Hall 158, 159, 165
Arnim, Elizabeth von 200
Arundel, Lord 33, 57
Ashcombe 239
Ashridge 122
Astor, William Waldorf 185
Athelhampton 226, 231
Aubrey, John 31
Augusta, Princess 103
Augustans 91
Austen, Jane 114, 121
Austen, Ralph 50

Bacon, Francis 22, 29, 30, 31, 36, 53, 165
Badminton 44, 108
Bakewell, Robert 42
Banks, Sir Joseph 102, 123
Barnsley 212, 235
Barry, Sir Charles 137, 138
Bartram, John 102
Basildon 95
Bateman, James 151, 152
Bateman, Richard 108
Batemans 246
Beaton, Donald 158
Beaufort, Duchess of 114
Beckford, William 94
Belsay 90, 103, 105
Belvoir 108
Benson, E. F. 206
Bettisfield 45
Biddulph 147, 151
Blenheim 74, 234
Blomfield, Sir Reginald 179, 182
Bobart, Jacob 45

Boleyn, Anne 185
Boscawen, Fanny 98
Botanic Garden, Oxford 45, 56
Botticelli 14
Boughton 42
Bowles, E. A. 147, 169, 226
Bowood 107, 108, 138, 192
Bramham 37
Bressingham 204
Bridgeman, Charles 64, 67, 72, 75
Brompton Park Nurseries 38, 60
Brooke, E. Adveno 138
Broughton Castle 215
Brown, Lancelot 'Capability' 94, 95, 98, 99,
    102, 103, 105, 107, 108, 109, 111, 116,
    120, 123, 138, 151, 179
Browne, Sir Thomas 50, 60
Bruce, Lady 85
de Bruyn 99
Buckingham, Duke of 41, 44
Buckland Monachorum 198, 219
Budding, Mr. 132, 154
Bulstrode 114
Burleigh, Lord 22, 30
Burlington, Lord 70, 82, 83, 86
Burne-Jones 164
Burney, Fanny 100
Buscot 231
Byron, Lord 90, 114

Campbell, Colen 75
Carew, Pole 121
Carlisle, Lord 74
Castle Howard 74, 125, 200, 201
Catherine of Braganza 38
Caus, Isaac de 36
Caus, Solomon de 30
Cavendish, George 15
Cecil family 55
Chalice, Mr. 123
Chambers, William 103, 105, 108, 132, 152
Charles I 15, 33, 36
Charles II 38
Charlton Park 237
Chastleton 26, 165
Chatsworth 43, 44, 64, 95, 128, 133, 143
Chaucer, Geoffrey 11
Chelsea Physic Garden 99, 101

Chicheley 87
China 103, 105, 116, 152
Chiswick House 62, 70, 71, 82, 86, 115, 122
Christ Curch, Oxford 54
Cibber, Colley 43
Claremont 74, 75, 78, 103
Claude 67, 77, 79, 83, 85, 91, 108, 109, 114
Clérisseau 105
Cleveland, Duchess of 108
Clifford daughters 136
Clive, Lord 103
Cliveden 41, 132, 158, 194
Cloisters Museum, N.Y. 14
Cobb 147
Cobbett, William 129, 133
Cobham, Lord 74, 86, 94
Colchester, Maynard 33
Colvin, Brenda 218
Columbines 22
Constable 114
Constable, William 114
Cook, Edward 151, 152
Cotehele 171
Cranborne Manor 17, 26, 29, 46, 51
Cromwell, Oliver 48
Crowe, Sylvia 218, 219, 235
Culpeper 204

Danby, Earl of 45
Danckwerts 42
Daniel, Friar Henry 14
Daniell, Thomas 112, 120
Dante 138
D'Arblay, M. 100
D'Argenville, Theory & Practice of
    Gardening 61, 138
Delany, Mrs. 114
Denmans 217
Digges, Sir Dudley 44
Disraeli 161, 244
Docwra's Manor 101, 202
Douglas, David 147
Drayton Green 127
Duchêne, Achille 234

Earle, Mrs. 173
East Ham 114
Eden, Garden of 13, 50, 53, 67

Eden, Emily 123
Ehret 114
East Lambrook Manor 226
Eliot, George 153, 154, 155, 244
Elizabeth I 13, 14, 22, 29
Ellacombe, Canon 158, 159, 169
Elliot, Brent 155
Elysium 57
Emes, William 98, 99
Enstone, Hermit of 36
Ewing, Mrs. 173

Fanshawe, Sir Harry 29
Farnborough Hall 60, 61
Faringdon House 12
Fish, Margery 219, 222, 226, 234, 235
Fitzgerald, Scott 200
Fleming, John 194
Flintham 102, 128, 130, 137, 143, 151, 187
Flitcroft, Henry 83
Florist's Societies 49
Fonthill 94
Foote, Samuel 99
Forrest 206
Fortune, Robert 151
Fothergill, Dr. John 114
Fountains Abbey 64, 75, 78
Frogmore 244

Gainsborough 91, 108, 109
Gaskell, Mrs. 153, 155
Gerard, the herbalist 14, 29
Gilpin, Rev. William 109
Giverny 177
Glendurgan 11, 146, 154
Goethe 71
Gravetye 169
Gray, Thomas 109
Gray's Inn 14
Great Dixter 13, 166
Grey's Court 17
Grimshaw, John Atkinson 158
Grimsthorpe Castle 204, 240, 247
Gurney, Mrs. 201

Ham House 42
Hamilton, Charles 86, 89, 94, 100, 107, 109, 114
Hampton, Dr.
    see Hill, Jason
Hampton Court 14, 15, 16, 26, 27, 29, 38, 42, 103, 108
Hanmer, Sir Thomas 45, 48
Harcourt, Lord 108
Hardwicke, Lord 75
Harlaxton Manor 159
Harvey, Dr. John 14, 100
Hatchlands 98
Hatfield 22, 29, 44, 45, 55, 192
Heale House 151, 164, 177, 237, 244
Helmingham Hall 20, 31, 191

Henrietta, Maria 36
Henry VIII 13, 15, 22, 26, 29, 238, 239
Hercules 79, 82, 103
    Temple of 83
Hestercombe 179, 180, 194
Het Loo 42
Hibberd, Shirley 133, 158
Hidcote 202, 207, 212, 214, 215, 218, 219, 226
Hill, Jason (alias Dr. Hampton) 215, 217, 218
Hill, Thomas (alias Didymus Mountain) 29, 238, 239
Hine, Thomas 151
Hoare, Henry 77, 78, 79, 82, 83, 85, 86, 94
Hogg, Thomas 152
Hole, Dean 159, 169
Holker 197
Homer 78
    Iliad 79
Hooker, Sir Joseph 151
Horace 67
Horticultural Society 123
Hortus Conclusus 12, 15
Huntington Botanic Gardens, California 14
Hussey, Christopher 95, 185
Hymas, Edward 155

Iford Manor 182, 185
India 120
Inkpen House 37
Institute of Landscape Architects 179

James I of Scotland 12, 15, 30
James IV of Scotland 29
James, Henry 164
James, John 61, 138
Jekyll, Miss 155, 158, 159, 165, 169, 173, 174, 177, 178, 180, 182, 186, 187, 191, 192, 194, 195, 207, 215, 244, 246
Jellicoe, Sir Geoffrey 218, 219, 226
Jennings, Mrs. 103
Johnson, Dr. 27, 86, 114
Johnston, Lawrence 207, 212, 214, 226
Jones, Henry 243
Jones, Inigo 33, 36

Keats, John 114
Kedleston 98
Kelmscott 164
Kent, William 59, 62, 64, 67, 70, 71, 72, 75, 95, 151
Kew 102, 103, 105, 108
Killerton 163, 206
Kingdon Ward 206
Kingston Lacy 38, 143
Knight, Richard Payne 108
Knightshayes 207
Knole 214

Langley, Batty 86, 99
Lawrence, D. H. 206

Lawrence, Mrs. 127
Lawson, William 165, 182
Le Nôtre 36, 37, 64, 69
Leonardslee 153
Levens Hall 26, 48, 49, 165
Linnaeus 135, 200
Little Haseley 22
Lloyd, Christopher 13, 166
Lloyd, Nathaniel 166
London, George 38, 42, 60, 244, 246
Longleat 26, 38
Loudon, Jane 128, 133, 187
Loudon, John Claudius 69, 71, 127, 132, 137, 154, 244
Louis XIV 61, 244
Lucas, Sir John of Colchester 54
Lyme Park 138
Lyttleton 86
Lutyens, Sir Edwin 178, 179, 180, 182, 186, 192, 197, 215

Magdalen College 45
Manners, Charles 109
Mansard 61
Markham, Gervase 182
Marlborough, Duke of 74
    Duchess of 85
Marvell, Andrew 50, 53
Mary Gardens 12
Mason, William 108
Mattei 83
    Choice of Hercules 82
Mawson, Thomas 179
Mayster, Jon le Gardener 237
Meader, James 98, 101, 132
Medici, Marie de 54
Melbourne Hall 37, 42, 69, 71
Metcalfe, Rev. Thomas 100, 101
Miller, Philip 99, 101
Milne, James Lees- 163
Milton, John 60
    Paradise Lost 67
Milton, Lord 95, 103
Milton Abbas 95, 103
Mitford, Miss 159, 161
Mitford, Nancy 222
Mollet, André 36, 37, 38
Monet, Claude 177
Montagu, Duke of 42
Moor Park 59
Morris, William 161, 163, 164, 169, 182
Mottisfont 25, 97, 186, 197, 208, 209, 217
Mountain, Didymus
    see Thomas Hill
Muskau, Prince Pückler 122
Munstead Wood 186
Myddleton House 226

National Trust 197, 247
Nesfield, William 132, 138
New College 16

Newby Hall 129, 132, 174
Newman 164
Newton, Lord 138
Nicolson, Harold 182, 215
Nonsuch 15, 17, 26
Northanger Abbey 109
Northbourne Court 123, 219
Northumberland, Earl of 26
    Duke of 98, 102
Nourse, Timothy 54
Nuneham Courtenay 108

Oare House 38, 100, 191, 242
Oatlands 44
Oliver, Sir Isaac 29
Ovid 53, 78
    Metamorphosis 79

Packwood 165
Page, Russell 219
Painshill 75, 89, 94, 102, 105, 109, 114
Palmer, Samuel 114
Pantheon, Stourhead 79, 82, 83
Papworth, John Buonarotti 128
Paradise Garden 12, 13, 16, 50
Parkinson, John 22, 27, 31, 50
Parkinson Society 173
Parterres Anglaises 42
Patte D'Oie 37, 53
Paul, William 133
Paxton, Joseph 128, 133, 143, 244
Peacock, Thomas Love 121
Pembroke, Earl of 36
Penjerrick 145
Pepys, Samuel 42
Peto, Harold 182, 185, 231
Petrarch 86, 138
Petre, Lord 108
Petworth 98
Philippa, Queen 19
Piranesi 105
Plato 85
Pliny 22
Pococke, Edward 54
Pope 64, 67, 70, 71, 85, 95
Portland, Duchess of 114, 115
Poussin 67, 77, 107, 109
Povey 36
Powis Castle 34, 165, 211, 222
Pre-Raphaelites 164
Prince, Uvedale 108
Prior, Matthew 64, 67
Prynne, William 50
Pulham, James 133

Radcliffe, Mrs. 114
Rea, John 48
Red House 164
Regent's Park 169
Reiss, Phyllis 212
Renishaw 194

Repton, Humphry 94, 95, 115, 116, 119,
    120, 121, 122, 125, 127, 138, 178, 179,
    182
Reynolds, Sir Joshua 74
Rievaulx 61, 81
Robins, Thomas 108, 237
Robinson, William 165, 169, 171, 178, 179,
    182, 186, 187, 192, 195, 207, 244
Rohde, Eleanor Sinclair 204
Rousham 59, 62, 70, 71, 72
Rousseau 90, 91, 99, 108
Royal Gardens 38
Ruskin 132, 161, 163, 164, 169, 182, 214
Russell, James 201
Russell Square 122
Rutland 109

Sackville-West, Vita 182, 207, 209, 211, 212,
    214, 215
St. James's Park 38
St. Mary-at- Lambeth 44
St. Paul's Walden Bury 37, 53
Saki 206
Salisbury, Earl of 44
Salvator Rosa 163
Sandby, Paul 108
Sayes Court 57
Sense & Sensibility 144
Serres 99
Shaftesbury, Lord 67, 82, 83, 90
Shakespeare 14, 22, 27, 29
Shaw, George Bernard 218
Shelburne, Lord 108
Shenstone, William 86
Sheringham 119
Shrublands 138, 143, 158
Shute House 117, 218, 222, 226, 234
Sidney, Sir Philip 54
Sissinghurst 22, 29, 182, 202, 207, 208, 211,
    215, 218, 219, 226
Sitwell, George 194
Sledmere 95
Socrates 82
Somerleyton Hall 116, 169
Southampton University 15, 19
Southcote, Philip 108
Spence, Joseph 108
Spenser 67
Stourhead 77, 78, 79, 83, 86, 94
Stowe 67, 70, 74, 82, 94
Studley Royal 61, 64, 75, 78, 79, 80, 91
Switzer, Stephen 60, 61, 67
Syon 98

Talman 42
Telfords of York 100
Temple, William 60, 105
    The Gardens of Epirus 59
Tennyson 137, 164
Theobalds 22, 30, 55
Thomas, Graham Stuart 112, 186, 234

Thomas, Kieth 206
Thompson, James 86
Tijou 42
Tintinhull 212, 215
Tradescant, John 44, 45
Trengwainton 147, 173, 226
Trentham 138, 158
Trollope, Anthony 164
Tunnard, Christopher 217, 218
Turner, William 22, 29
Turner 182
Tusser, Thomas 29, 54

Unicorn Tapestries 14
Upcher, Abbot 119

Vanbrugh 64, 67, 74, 75, 85
Van Nost 42, 69
Veitch, Messrs. 147
Venus 86
Versailles 42, 61, 69, 143, 244
Victoria, Queen 127, 163, 169, 244
Virgil 67, 78, 83, 85, 86
    Aeneid 79

Waller, Edmund 75
Wallington 161
Walpole, Horace 67, 70, 74, 85, 105
    History of the Modern Taste
    in Gardening 64
Ward, Kingdon 112, 152, 154
Ware, Samuel 155
Warley 178
West Green House 243, 244
West Wycombe 85, 92, 99
Westbury Court 33, 36
White, Gilbert 102, 103
Whitehall Palace 38, 244
Whitton 102
Wilde, Oscar 161
Wilderness 50
William & Mary 33, 42, 244
Willmott, Miss 178
Willoughby, Sir Francis 30
Wilton 36, 82, 123
Wimbledon Manor 36
Windsor 12, 237
Wise, Henry 60, 64, 69, 71
Worsley, Cardinal 14, 15
Woodbridge, Kenneth 85
Woods, Richard 99
Wordsworth, William 80, 91, 114
World, The 86
Wotton, Sir Henry 29
Wressle 26
Wright, Thomas 108

Xenophon
    Memorabilia 82, 83

Yonge, Charlotte, M. 137

·DHF·